HONDA—
THE EARLY
CLASSIC
MOTORCYCLES

OSPREY
COLLECTOR'S
LIBRARY

HONDA—
THE EARLY
CLASSIC
MOTORCYLCES

All the singles, twins and fours, including production racers and Gold Wing—1947 to 1977

Roy Bacon

Published in 1985 by Osprey Publishing Limited
12–14 Long Acre, London WC2E 9LP
Member company of the George Philip Group

British Library Cataloguing in Publication Data

Bacon, Roy H.
    Honda—the early classic motorcycles: all
    singles, twins and fours from 1945 to the
    Gold Wing in 1974.—(Osprey collector's
    library)
    1. Honda motorcycle—History
    I. Title
    629.2'275   TL448.H6
ISBN 0-85045-596-0

Editor Tim Parker
Filmset and printed in England by
BAS Printers Limited, Over Wallop, Hampshire

Contents

Foreword by Tommy Robb 7

Acknowledgements 8

1 Clip-ons, Dreams and Benlys 10

2 Step-thru and all those 'nice people' 23

3 Twins in all sizes 61

4 Four—what a bombshell! 91

5 On a Wing or a prayer 115

6 Racers for sale 127

7 Factory competition 145

Appendices

1 Specifications—Singles 164

  Twins 176

  Fours 183

  Production road racers 185

2 Model recognition 186

3 Model chart 188

Tommy Robb (8) leads Tom Phillis (5) during the 1962
125 TT. The gallant and skilful Robb finished second with
Phillis third; Luigi Taveri won at a race speed of
144·64 km/h. The race was fast

Foreword by Tommy Robb

My first association with the Honda Motor Company was 23 years ago, in 1962, when I was one of the privileged few to be chosen as a 'works rider' and their Junior bike enabled me to finish runner-up in that year's 350 cc World Championship.

Honda, even then, was one of the greatest names ever to hit the road racing scene and was already developing engines that were technically years ahead of their time. Sochirio Honda and his team were unable to understand the meaning of the word defeat, and this was proved over and over again in the manner with which they approached the motorcycle development scene—both in racing and touring machines.

An example of this dedication and disregard for expense came to us at the start of the 1962 season when the 50 Honda singles were ridden in the first World Championship event, the Spanish Grand Prix at Montjuich Park, by Kunimitsu Takahashi, Luigi Taveri and myself. At the end of the event Suzukis were 1st, 2nd and 4th, and we were 3rd, 5th and 6th on our Hondas. When asked why we didn't occupy the first three positions the Japanese manager was informed that our six-speed ohc four-strokes were no match on acceleration for the rapid two-strokes of the Japanese opposition. We were then asked what we would need to win and in unison, in three different languages, we chorused eight-speed gearboxes. The following week was the French Grand Prix, followed a week later by TT practice. In the manager's hotel bedroom we plotted the ratios required for an eight-speed gearbox. A three-hour telephone call to Tokyo followed, outlining the reason for our failure that day and what we considered to be the cure. Two weeks later, in the middle of practice week, three new 50 cc engines were flown in, complete with eight-speed gearboxes and more power. The outcome was that Ernst Degner won the race, with Luigi 2nd and myself 3rd. We had proved

that we were heading in the right direction and only one of the works Suzukis finished in front. Another 'high power' meeting, more telephone calls to Japan, and at Assen—the Dutch TT, three weeks later—three more brand new machines turned up complete with ten-speed gearboxes.

This was a typical example of the speed and dedication with which the Honda factory acted upon anything which would improve their racing machines and consequently their road bikes.

Today, four-cylinder machines are 'old hat' and can be seen in hundreds of cities all over the world. However, in those days only certain works teams had fours, and the true meaning of the word nostalgia is to listen to an open-piped Honda Four hurtling down the mountain from Creg-ny-Baa towards Hilberry at 14,000 rpm.

This book, superbly written in explicit detail by Roy Bacon, details not only the rise of the Honda motorcycle from a humble beginning to its current fame, but also gives an in-depth description of nearly every machine ever produced at the famous factory in Japan. Apart from giving superb technical details on models of which some readers will never even have heard, there is a complete specification listing which even includes the production racers of the mid-sixties, which will be of particular interest to classic racing enthusiasts.

As a director of my own motorcycle company, I am still proud to be a 'Honda specialist' and carry with me, even today, sparkling memories of those classic Honda days.

Tommy Robb
250 cc British Champion 1962
350 cc World Championship runner-up 1962
500 cc Irish Champion 1958, 1959, 1960
Currently still connected with Honda as the managing director of his own Honda dealership in Warrington, Cheshire
December 1984

Acknowledgements

A Honda motorcycle first came into my life during practice for the 1962 TT when I was offered a ride on a race-kitted CB92. Very interesting, although it was used in the race by another rider with greater problems than I. Next was a hired C100 and later many others including a couple bought for commuting in and around London.

One of the highlights of Honda riding was on long-time friend Mole Benn's CR110. So cramped that it took two goes to get my feet on the rests, and so light and dainty to handle. All those gears and all those revs took some getting used to as well.

Mole helped me greatly in writing this book, with information on the racer and on the first CB750—he had a 1969 model. Other good friends who assisted on the production racer side were Alf Briggs, the font of CR knowledge in the UK, and Richard Renstrom from the USA, who guided me to Larry Johnson of Oregon. Larry is the US font of CR data and has an incredible collection of four machines, one of each size, all beautifully restored as can be seen in the photographs he kindly lent me.

On the road machines Brian O'Reily has helped me many times over the years answering my queries to enable me to do my readers' agony column. For this project he kindly lent me material and accepted the chore of reading and checking the manuscript.

For pictures I again turned to my friends at the magazines. Many of these pictures were made available thanks to the good offices of Ron Beacham who is i/c the EMAP archives, which now hold the old *Motor Cycle Weekly* files. Some pictures were taken from brochure material and others came from press kits accumulated over the years. The National Motor Museum at Beaulieu again assisted with material and Mole Benn lent me more from his private collection.

A number of pictures were taken by the professional and work used came from A'Court Photographs, Allsport, D. J. Crawford, F. G. N. Ewence, Jan Hesse, Douglas Jackson, Roy Keirby, Manx Press Pictures, Newcombe and Johnson, Nick Nicholls, Bill Salmond and Sport & General.

As usual the pictures were returned to their source and I have tried to make contact to clear copyright. If my letter failed to reach you or I have used an unmarked print without knowing this, I can only apologize.

To end I must thank my old friend Tommy Robb (28 times in the top six places in two years of World Championship Grands Prix aboard works Hondas) for writing the foreword and for his kind remarks to me just after I had ridden in my first TT in 1962. He was second and I a late finisher in the 125 race; we sat on the wall by the circuit and chatted while the 350 race ran its course.

And of course my friends at Osprey without whom it would not get done. With 14 titles it could easily slip, but Tim Parker makes sure it does not.

Roy Bacon
Niton, Isle of Wight
October 1984

1 | Clip-ons, Dreams and Benlys

Part of a 1973 advertisement which says it all and depicts the founder, the model A and the Honda Technical Research Institute in 1947

The Honda Motor Company is the largest producer of motorcycles in the world and has held that number one position for many years. It was not always so, for they came from obscurity, building a few crude machines each day, like so many other similar tiny firms. In a decade they swamped Japan, in two the world.

The man whose name the company bears, and who began it, is one Soichiro Honda, who was born in 1906, the eldest son of a blacksmith, in the small village of Komyo, a place long since swallowed up by the expansion of the city of Hamamatsu. From an early age he was interested in machinery of all types and at school took a practical approach to things that he liked and ignored his books—ways that were to stay with him for much of his working life.

At 16 he left school and went into the car trade as an apprentice at one of the few repair shops in Tokyo. In 1923 this was one of the thousands of buildings wrecked by a major earthquake and in the ensuing period of rebuilding and repairing Honda learned a great deal. He returned to Hamamatsu in 1928 to put his new-found knowledge to use in his own repair shop and, after an initial struggle, became established and built up his business.

This prospered well enough for him to indulge in racing with some success until the All-Japan Automobile Speed Championships in 1937, when a bad crash put him out and into hospital. Once recovered he decided to try a new line as a manufacturer of piston rings and in this his lack of technical knowledge caused him to come badly unstuck. Piston rings look simple enough to make, but in truth involve complex metallurgy and special manufacturing techniques. Honda's practical skills enabled him to overcome the problems of getting the finished part into the correct shape and to the tight tolerances, but the first was another matter and he was forced to seek guidance from the local technical college.

With their help he managed to find a suitable material for his piston rings and went on to produce them in large numbers. The lesson had not been lost, however, and he went on to study metallurgy at the college for two years. Having thus equipped himself with information vital to his product he then set himself the job of making it faster and with peasant labour. In this he was very skilled, with no need of tutors, and during the war years developed equipment to mass produce piston rings and later to machine, at high speed, the curves of a propeller.

In 1944 his factory was heavily bombed and early in the next year the remnants were razed to the ground by an earthquake. The end of the war came for Soichiro Honda as he and his men struggled to repair their machines. He sold out and for the rest of 1945 and much of 1946 sat back, enjoyed himself and looked for a new business to interest him.

In October 1946 he founded the Honda Technical Research Institute in Hamamatsu. Now, such a title produces an image of a multi-million dollar establishment stretching over many acres. Then, the title may have been impressive, but the reality was an 18 by 12 foot wooden shed. It fitted in well in the chaos that was postwar Japan with its bankrupt economy and nearly dead industry.

Transport was the thing, thought Honda, for cars and motorcycles were seldom far from his mind. At a time when petrol was rationed and acutely short, people struggled with trains and trams and had no alternative but to put up with the crush. Bicycles were popular but hard work over any distance, so a small motorcycle simply had to succeed, for it would give mobility at minimal cost and use little fuel.

It was not an original idea, but Honda put it to work. He found 500 surplus army engines, either Tohatsu or Mikuni units, and he and a small team of men worked in the shed to fit them to bicycles with a belt drive to the rear wheel. He also devised a fuel using turpentine extracted from pine trees and mixed it with petrol to eke the latter out. It was anything but volatile so starting was haphazard, and once the engine did respond to frantic pedalling it emitted dense clouds of acrid smoke.

But it was better than walking, unless wind or gradient were against you, and the 500 engines were quickly used up, so Honda designed his own, and to make sure it would work he did what any sensible designer would have done in his place and copied the ex-army unit. This first engine was sometimes called the chimney due to the height of the cylinder and its head, also due to the fumes that came from its exhaust when the turpentine and petrol fuel mixture was used, but by November 1947 it had been developed into the A type engine unit.

The first Honda engine was a single-cylinder two-stroke of 50 cc which developed 1 bhp at 5000 rpm. The cylinder was vertical with the exhaust bolted to the front and a decompressor above it in the cylinder head sited opposite the rear-mounted spark plug. The carburettor was a slide type and bolted to the base of the crankcase with a valve to control the induction process. A flywheel magneto on the left provided ignition.

The engine unit was built with a reduction gear to a countershaft and from this a belt drove the rear wheel with a jockey pulley to maintain the tension. The whole assembly fitted within the frame of a standard gent's bicycle, to which it was clamped with the fuel tank perched on the top tube. The exhaust ran down to a small

silencer mounted on the left beside the rear wheel and in all other respects that first machine was pure pedal cycle.

Not so a later variant. This retained the same engine and belt drive but mounted it in a stronger but heavier frame which owed something to the early motorcycle industry. The result was lower and longer, with the pedals further back and the engine lower. The frame was laid out like a cycle, but stretched out with a horizontal bracing tube beneath the top one.

Front suspension was provided, but of the rocking girder type first used on Triumph machines in 1906. Just as on the English machine the fork member pivoted about the lower headrace and was controlled by a horizontally mounted barrel spring attached to the fork top and the handlebar stem. Very small drum brakes were fitted, a better saddle tank carried the fuel and a veteran type of saddle with downhung tension support springs was used.

In 1948 Honda built his B model, which followed a very different concept, for it had three

Variant of the model A with rocking girder front fork and other veteran features

wheels, two at the rear, and a large cargo bin behind the rider. It was a style much used in Italy for the carriage of trade goods, but there it was normally towed along by a 500 cc ohv engine coupled to a four-speed gearbox. Honda made do with a stretched version of the A engine of 89 cc capacity and with a rear exhaust port to suit the installation. It produced 1·2 bhp at 4500 rpm and still drove the rear wheel by belt with pedalling gear to help out when needed.

The B model frame was in channel steel and carried its front wheel in light girder forks. The frame members splayed out low down to run back under the bin and because of this the pedals were set within them, hung from a central bicycle frame that still supported the engine.

In that same year the C model was built using the same 89 cc engine, but with front exhaust

and improved to give 3 bhp at 3000 rpm. The cycle parts were also improved from the second A model by the adoption of girder forks with a central spring and the later style of compression springs for the saddle.

It was still fitted with belt drive and still a very crude machine, but so were many others in Japan at that time. So, in September 1948, Soichiro founded the Honda Motor Company, to join the list of manufacturers of whom, at that point, there were not many, for some of the pre-war ones such as Cabton did not get back into production until 1949, the year in which they made the grand total of 19 machines.

Japanese motorcycle production had always been in small numbers up until then and was to stay that way for a year or two more. Their best year had been 1940, when 3037 machines were built, but most of these had been Rikuo copies of the Harley-Davidson. The industry itself did date back a long way (to 1908) and had managed to survive fluctuating fortunes in a country where many still travelled by boat.

The model C with the 89 cc engine from the B, girder forks and a more modern saddle

Around 1930 the motorcycle industry and, in fact, Japanese industry as a whole benefited from the purchase of the rights to build an obsolete Harley-Davidson. It became the Rikuo and in itself was none too important, although some 18,000 were built in the period up to 1945. What mattered was the information that came with the engineering drawings on steel heat treatment, materials, mass production, precision, interchangeable parts, workshop cleanliness and the assembly line tricks needed to build complex machines in large numbers.

At the time Japan was in the throes of military expansion, which was to lead to the dominance of the military in the government. They demanded and got the motorized transport they wanted along with much else and in the process advanced Japanese industry.

By 1945 any such gains were lost in the rubble of defeat, but from this sprang the need for transport and the beginnings of an infant industry. It built 127 motorcycles in 1945 and 211 in 1946, hardly figures to make any real impact among Japan's teeming millions. Early makes were Showa, Tohatsu, Pointer, Fuji and Mitsubishi, to be quickly joined by many more in those early, tumultuous postwar days of American occupation and black marketeering.

For the masses anything with wheels and an engine was another machine and therefore desirable, but Honda was already looking ahead of the crude devices to better things. At that point no one made both their own engine and frame, but late in 1949 he changed that with his model D, the first Honda Dream. For all his aspirations it was still crude, but it was the first complete postwar machine to be built by one firm.

The engine of the model D was still a two-stroke, but the capacity was up to 98 cc and the bore and stroke were equal at 50 mm. The exhaust port was at the rear of the cylinder and connected by pipe to a silencer mounted low down on the right alongside the rear wheel. The carburettor went in front of the crankcase, which it fed via a valve, and the mixture was ignited by a flywheel magneto mounted on the right end of the crankshaft. The primary transmission went on the left and, via a clutch, drove a two-speed gearbox built onto the rear of the engine. The gears were selected by a rocking pedal on the left and the engine started by a kickstarter on the right. The final drive was on the left by chain

The first complete machine built by one firm postwar, the model D and the first Honda Dream

Transport for the masses and the first commercial foundation stone, the model F Cub which bolted to any bicycle in minutes

under a guard. Both hubs had drum brakes and the front was carried in a neat pair of telescopic forks. The frame was constructed of channel steel, so was fairly substantial and at first was without any rear suspension.

The machine's appearance was rather old-fashioned and European, for the tank was set into the top frame member and the headlamp stuck out on a pair of light stays. The rider was provided with a saddle and a rear carrier on which to strap his goods. Under the seat went a cylindrical toolbox.

Crude it may have been, but in broad outline it was much as many European models at that time and perhaps better than some English auto-cycles. In Japan it was a good machine and was soon selling well, but this very success produced

a problem outside the usual easily remedied mechanical ones, and Honda could not solve it quite so quickly.

This was finance. The expansion of the company had been haphazard and many of the outlets were small bicycle shops. This was an excellent means of reaching customers for the A engine, but not so good for Honda's cash flow. Many of these small firms could and would vanish overnight with debts unpaid, and others were slow, too slow, to settle their accounts.

The company needed someone to sort this confusion out and to control the sales and finance while Soichiro concentrated on his beloved machinery. He found the man he needed in Takeo Fujisawa, who joined him and quickly overcame the dealer problems. Takeo then looked at their models and their opposition and his message to Soichiro was simple—we must have a four-stroke, as this makes a pleasant sound as it runs, not the nasty high-pitched note of the two-stroke.

While Honda the technician was thinking about this the company opened an office in Tokyo early in 1950. This put them firmly in the centre of Japanese commerce and later in that year a new plant was completed in northern Tokyo. Into it went machinery bought with a government loan, and production was stepped up from 20 to 300 machines a month. In comparison with later figures even this increase seems minor until compared with the total Japanese motorcycle production figure for 1950, which amounted to 2633 machines. About 1000 of this number were Hondas and the remaining 1600 were shared between nine other companies.

Around the same time Fujisawa changed the dealer set-up from some 200 outlets in the Hamamatsu area to 5000 sales and service points nationwide. No one else offered this blanket cover and it quickly began to pay off as the volume pulled the price down and the availability of spares and service persuaded people to buy Honda rather than some smaller, more local make.

Japanese motorcycle production jumped to 11,510 in 1951 and the first signs of the great price war began to materialize. For this Honda continued with the D type and worked on his first four-stroke. This was to be the E model Dream and was designed at a time when his business rivals were presenting a petition to the government to discourage imports. Honda refused to go along with this and, alone, held to his belief that a better product, good service and the right price would ensure a company's success.

In truth it was not the first time the minute Japanese industry had needed help and protection, for in the early 1920s they had very nearly vanished under a flood of imports. Then, the government had brought in The Military Vehicle Subsidy Law, which benefited makers or owners of any motor vehicles that might be suitable for military use; provided it was made in Japan. This was enough to interest a number of good-sized companies in motorcycles, one of which in time became Meguro, later taken over by Kawasaki, one of Japan's motorcycle big four. Unfortunately for the country's balance of payments in the 1920s none of the Japanese machines could hold a candle to the imports for power, reliable running or spares fitting, so the scheme went sideways rather than forwards. In time this led to the Harley-Davidson copy and by the late 1930s a few more firms were producing small numbers of machines.

In the early fifties the first effect of the efforts of Cabton, Tohatsu, Miyata, IMC and Fuji was a stiff tariff wall to keep the imports at bay. Honda ignored this and went on with his model E, and in July 1951 the prototype was tested on the run up the Hakone Mountains. The rider was Kiyoshi Kawashima, who had joined Soichiro in March 1947 and had worked with him to develop the E. He was followed up the pass by Soichiro and Takeo in a car and at the summit the three Japanese knew they had a good machine.

Honda's first four-stroke had a single-cylinder engine of 146 cc producing 5·5 bhp at 5000 rpm. The valves were in the cylinder head and there were three of them, two inlet and one exhaust. All were opened by a camshaft located high up in the crankcase, aft of the crankshaft, with push-rods which ran up in a tunnel cast into the back of the cylinder. On top of the head a large domed cover enclosed the valve gear. Two carburettors were fitted on splayed ports and a single exhaust pipe ran low on the right to the silencer.

A two-speed gearbox was built in unit with the engine and drove the rear wheel by chain. The unit was housed in a channel steel frame with duplex loops and either rigid rear or plunger suspension, the whole thing being very much on the lines of the rigid model D. Telescopic front forks were fitted and both wheels had drum brakes. The bulk of the remaining detail fittings were as used on the D model, so the saddle and inset fuel tank continued.

The appearance of these early Honda models was much like pre-war German machines and so very old-fashioned by European standards. The resulting E model might have been a good motorcycle for Japan in 1951, but even there the handling was thought poor and the oil consumption heavy. For all that it nevertheless sold well, for it was reasonably reliable and spares that would fit were available all over Japan. So riders bought the Honda and production increased to 130 machines per day—a Japanese record.

While this was a good thing, the E was a true motorcycle and as such pitched above most people's levels of both performance and cost. For the masses something smaller and cheaper was required and such was the development of Japan's economy at that time that this meant a clip-on engine for a bicycle. For Honda this was a new challenge. He sought to build something far better than the crude model A with its belt drive and cumbersome appearance.

The result in June 1952 was the F model Cub, a 50 cc unit that could be fitted in minutes to any standard bicycle. For this Honda went back to a two-stroke with a single horizontal cylinder. It produced 1 bhp at 3000 rpm with a reduction gear behind the crankcase and a small silencer below the complete unit. The flywheel magneto went on the left of the engine and the whole unit was hung low down to the left side of the rear wheel.

A sprocket at the rear of the unit was coupled by chain to a larger one clipped to the rear wheel and a drum-like fuel tank attached to the rear seat stay. The whole assembly added only 6 kg to the machine weight and they were just what was wanted. Sales were so good that production reached 6500 per month by October that year and the Cub accounted for 70 per cent of Japanese motorcycle production that month.

That same year Honda began exporting in a very small way in the South-East Asia area, but the numbers were minimal, for there was little need to ship abroad as the home market swallowed all he could produce with the equipment he had. The transport famine in Japan was just as rife and brought in many more manufacturers who craved a slice of the market. That market was large and well protected, but within the tariff walls a price war raged and was fought to the Eastern code of no prisoners. It continued throughout the 1950s and decimated the ranks of makers. From over 100 they fell to 50, then 20, then 10 to 8 and in the 1960s shrank to the big four.

Honda was in the forefront of this war, cutting down competitors by the score, and the key to their success lay in investment and a crisis. The investment was in machine tools and came late in 1952. Soichiro was well aware of the shortcomings of his equipment and the limitations this placed on design, production and quality. Machining processes took far too long to complete and were often hit-and-miss, so were woefully inadequate for his dreams of worldwide sales of first-class machines.

So he went on a trip to Europe and the USA to look at motorcycles and machine tools. He was impressed, more than that he was overawed by the wealth of expertise he saw in Germany and Italy in particular, and by the equipment he saw which could grind out parts at a rate unheard of in Japan.

He went, he saw, he bought—to the tune of over one million dollars (in 1952–53) and he bought the latest, the most up-to-date machine tools. He lacked the cash to pay for them, but happily thought Takeo would take care of that by selling more motorcycles. After all, he reasoned, the new tools would enable the price to be cut, that would help to sell more machines, increased production would haul the price even lower and more competitors would commit *hara-kiri*. What he left out of his calculation was the end of the Korean War and the disappearance of the US orders and GI money as their war effort dispersed back to the States.

Before this affected the company Soichiro was awarded the Medal of Honour with Blue Ribbon for his contribution to Japan's postwar recovery and it is said that he had to buy a suit for the presentation by the Emperor. The son of a blacksmith preferred working clothes and lacked formal attire.

His award was cited in the 1952 honours list, and that year saw the start of production of the H engine for agricultural use. The next year brought another motorcycle, the J type, which was also the first of the Benly models, sometimes called Benri. The machine was Honda's first, good, modern motorcycle and was built alongside the Dream, which became the model 3E, and which apart from acquiring a three-speed gearbox kept its pre-war appearance and performance.

The J was very different and a very close copy of the contemporary lightweight NSU from West Germany. It had a single-cylinder, 89 cc, overhead-valve engine which produced 3·8 bhp at 6000 rpm. This was built in unit with a three-speed gearbox with a positive stop footchange operated by the left foot. The kickstart pedal also went on the left, while the rear brake was on the right.

The frame was like the NSU, a spine type built up from two pressings welded together. Holes in the pressings accommodated the electrics, the tool-kit and the air cleaner, while suspension was by telescopics and a rear fork controlled by a torsion member. The single saddle was canti-levered out, a pillion pad or rear carrier went on top of the rear mudguard and a saddle tank was fitted.

Suddenly Honda had an up-to-date model that was as modern as the best in Europe in styl-ing even if the power output was a little down on German products. It was a success, but as 1953 drew to a close, the Japanese economy faltered and Honda faced a money crisis.

The next six months was a desperate time for Honda and his associates as they battled against a merger with Mitsubishi, whose bank was the company's main creditor. The workforce backed the top men's investment in machine tools to the hilt by working round the clock, without holidays and sometimes without pay. Executives went out and chased the money into the com-pany and somehow the installments were paid.

Fortunately for Honda there were far-sighted men in the bank who could look further ahead than the immediate cash-flow crisis. They argued against a foreclosure, for they saw that the money for the tools was eventually going to come and that the tools themselves were a first-class asset. With their help Honda rode out the financial storm and emerged into calmer waters with the company strengthened by the exper-ience. They now knew without doubt that invest-ment paid off provided you kept to your plan.

Despite the money problems Honda did not hold back in the design area and early in 1954 announced his first scooter, the model K, or Juno. At first this was fitted with a 200 cc engine, but this was soon enlarged to dimensions of 70 × 57 mm and 219 cc for the single-cylinder.

The valves were overhead and the engine was coupled to a three-speed gearbox which drove the rear wheel by an enclosed chain.

The machine was of the conventional scooter format with small wheels and enclosure of the mechanics, but in appearance copied the rather heavy and ponderous German style. The front suspension was by leading links and the rear a pivoted fork. The body had a tunnel from the apron to the engine cover, so lacked the flat floor and light looks of the Italian scooters. This was accentuated by the seats, which were fitted direct on the body top, and an immense wind-screen. This had stays and side panels with heavy looks and a further screen which could be moun-ted above the first or stowed in front of it.

The screen was static, so the bars moved behind it, and just below it, in the front panel, were set turn indicators. These were matched at the rear by lights faired into the side-panelling. All told it was an impressive machine.

Along with the scooter came two enlarged variations of older models. The first was the 4E, which was still cast in the likeness of its earlier mould and so retained its old-fashioned looks. The capacity went up to 220 cc, which raised the power a little, but otherwise the machine con-tinued with its three speeds, channel frame, tele-scopics and plunger rear. Some attempt was made to improve the looks by cowling the head-light, and the cylinder head had its exhaust port on the left, so the pipe and silencer also went on that side. Its production continued into 1955, but it was then dropped, for the firm had pro-gressed to much better things.

The second enlargement for 1954 was the JA, which continued the NSU theme and German looks. The internal engine dimensions became 60 × 49 mm to give 138 cc and this raised the power a little while reducing the engine speed. It continued with overhead valves and three speeds, while the exhaust pipe was shielded for its initial run.

The frame stayed as a spine type built up from

pressings and the suspension continued with telescopics and pivoted fork but with the latter controlled by a pair of spring units. The general fittings were little altered from those of the model J.

That same year saw a Dream running in a race in Brazil, for Honda believed in the advertising power of racing. The speed bug in him had lain dormant since pre-war days, but was struggling to emerge and had encouraged him to enter the Nagoya TT the previous year. It also took him to the Isle of Man TT in 1954 and he returned despairing but determined. The despair came from the realization that his machines lagged far behind the German and Italian designs that were winning the races, that his road models lacked the sophistication of Europe, that components such as magnetos, plugs, carburettors, tyres and much more were far more developed there. The determination was to return and win, win on the race circuits and in the showrooms.

To this end he took home all manner of components to study and analyse. In Japan the government continued to encourage their home manufacturers and not just with the import tariffs and a commodity tax. They instigated a buy Japanese campaign and soon all government agencies bought home machines only and this alone kept many firms going.

In 1955 the general importation of foreign machines was halted by currency control. To buy abroad the private citizen had to change his yen into pounds sterling, dollars, lire or marks in order to obtain a bank draft to pay for the machine. The banks could and would refuse to do this; it was illegal to take yen out of the country so the citizen was stymied. He either bought Japanese or walked; which made for a large, docile home market.

The exception to these rules was the home manufacturer. If Honda, or any of the others, wished to import a Guzzi, DKW or BSA for study then the government waived the rules, dispensed with the duties and would help with a

Above **A 1953 advertisement for the first Honda Benly known as the model J. The firm's first modern motorcycle**

Top **The real thing, the J. Still much like an NSU at this stage**

loan if required. Honda, and the others, learned quickly from these lessons and at first copied and then improved.

The price war went on and by now Honda were dominating the market and calling the tune. Their factories were modern and equipped with the latest and best machine tools from the West, mainly American, German and Swiss. Production quantities were large and the economics of scale enabled them to undercut most firms. It was ferocious for a while with small companies dropping like flies, but gradually the industry reshaped itself into a small number of large and very capable firms. Then in time these came down to four. Tohatsu folded as a result of a strike, Showa over-engineered and ran out of money, Bridgestone went back to making tyres for the others and Shin Meiwa let the Pointer die off.

Before this was finished Japan was the leading maker of motorcycles and their design was improving beyond the best they had copied. As the 1950s drew to a close their designers settled into a more stable life pattern. Before then they were often forced to skip from firm to firm as these folded, but always learning new designs, new techniques and new processes. Once they found a well-managed and secure company they dug in and began to exploit the wealth of experience they had gathered along the way.

By that time the Japanese market was saturated. No longer could they expect to find new customers at home in the sense of expanding the market. As teenagers became customers so the older riders moved on to cars and the numbers balanced. Machines were replaced of course, but it was time to look elsewhere, abroad, at America and Europe.

And outside Japan they were unknown. They ground out three-quarters of a million machines in 1959 and were thought of as a joke in the West. It was to become a joke with a bitter twist.

As the Japanese industry sorted itself out and moved towards the day it would start exporting in real numbers, Honda pushed ahead with his new designs. The Benly became the JB, with a slight reduction in capacity to 125 cc and a styled nacelle for the headlight. Late in 1955 it was further modified as the JC, and although the capacity remained at 125 cc the power went up and a four-speed gearbox was fitted. More to be noticed were the front forks, which became long leading links of the Earles type with twin spring units. The front mudguard was changed to a massive, well-valanced, sprung type and this did nothing to enhance the appearance, as was usual with this design.

Of far more interest in the spring of 1955 was the Dream SA, for this was Honda's first overhead camshaft model and his first with four speeds, as it preceded the JC by a few months. The SA had a single-cylinder engine of 246 cc set vertically in the frame with the gearbox built in unit with it. The camshaft was driven by a chain which ran in a tunnel cast in the right side of both head and barrel. The ports were angled so that the carburettor pointed to the right and the exhaust pipe to the left, from where it ran down to a low-mounted silencer on that side.

The engine unit looked very clean, with polished covers on each side and the gearbox section maintained the nice lines. The whole unit went into a spine-type frame built up from pressings with the addition of a down tube to support its front. Suspension was by telescopic forks at the front and pivoted fork at the rear and both hubs were of the full-width, light alloy type. The rear chain went on the right and was fully enclosed and the wheels were shrouded by substantial mudguards. The rear one was made as a continuation of the main frame and the whole machine retained some of the German lines of the Benly models.

This was enhanced by the cantilever saddle, rear carrier and headlamp nacelle, but not by the lines of the engine. From some angles this had a style that was to be seen again and again in years to come on twins in particular, while from other points the line remained very much European.

Along with the SA, Honda introduced the larger SB of 344 cc. It produced a little more power but was otherwise a replica of the smaller machine in most respects. The one noticeable difference lay in the exhaust pipe, which on the SB swelled out from the port and then contracted back to the normal pipe size to run back to the silencer.

These two models were both significant in their own ways. The 250 was the first Honda camshaft engine and before building it Honda had a good look at the Showa and the servicing prob-

lems that machine had suffered. These had centred on oil leaks and cam chain breakage and had become a nightmare for their dealers. The 350 was significant, for with it Honda moved out of the commuter market and into the sports one. It was a major step.

In 1957 the camshaft singles became the ME and MF with increased power outputs and new front forks. The forks looked much like tele-

A scooter excursion, the model KB from 1955 with single-cylinder engine and massive bodywork

The first overhead camshaft Honda was the 246 cc model SA which appeared in 1955. It was joined by the similar 344 cc SB

scopics, but were in truth hydraulically damped leading links. The pivot point was formed in a housing at the base of each fork leg and lay just behind it. The short link ran forward to clamp onto the wheel spindle and its pivot carried a shorter arm within the housing. The forward end of this was formed into a cup which carried the lower end of a pushrod which in turn transmitted the wheel movement to a spring concealed within the telescopic leg. In addition a further arm ran down to move a piston within a horizontal cylinder machined into the base of the housing and thus provided the hydraulic damping.

A torque arm connected the brake backplate to a pivot behind the fork leg and the brake cable swept in from behind on the left to connect to the single leading shoe drum brake in the full-width hub.

A substantial front mudguard was fitted and had a massive flare at the rear. The front tapered down and managed to avoid the usual heavy appearance normally associated with this design. In other respects the two new models were as the earlier ones down to the shape of the side panels that enclosed the electrics, tools and air cleaner on the right.

In all, the M models had nice lines and only the single seat, rear carrier and resulting exposed frame remained of the German style. Honda was now moving forward in his designs to lead his country and the world—soon his ambition would take him overseas. Before that happened though he did have one radical machine to finalize and his first move to improved power output with more cylinders.

Super Cubs and Twins were waiting in the wings to take on the world.

2 | Step-thru and all those 'nice people'

The first rule for all companies is that of survival and to do this they have to show a profit. Just what the definition of profit is seems to vary from country to country, indeed from accountant to accountant, but in Japan in 1958 it meant having a cash surplus each year. The sales volume and the amount of money made from it can vary a great deal, but certain guidelines do emerge from a study of firms large and small even if there are exceptions.

A small firm can specialize and often this allows them to make their product very well but in limited numbers. For a large firm to attempt this without other items in their range would be foolhardy as the balance of expertise, cash flow and volume would be all wrong. What a large firm needs is a nice, steady, easily produced commodity that will give them a broad financial base. This will then allow them to investigate the more exotic without financial trauma. For a small firm to attempt this could be dangerous as a mass-produced product has to be right and fully developed before production starts. Errors that appear later can finish a firm due to the sheer volume of numbers that need correcting.

By the mid-1950s Soichiro Honda was running a big firm. His base product was the Cub, which was churned out in large numbers, but he could see that the public taste and purse was ready to move on. In postwar Europe the trend of sequence was to run first a bicycle, then a clip-on, moped, scooter, bubble-car, small car and

YOU
MEET THE
NICEST
PEOPLE
ON A HONDA
世界の
ナイセスト
ピープル
ホンダ
に乗る

finally a large car. The motorcycle did not figure in this train to prosperity for Mr Average. It was used and enjoyed by a minority and later became far more socially accepted, a fun machine and a household second or third vehicle.

What Honda sought was a next step on from the Cub, something complete and not just an add-on to someone else's bicycle. Nothing too

The slogan that sold motorcycling and Honda to a new public all over the world

The start of the Super Cub, the 1958 C100

large or pricey for it had to sell everywhere right round the world. Nothing too complex, for to sell in quantity it would have to win the market of developing countries which lacked sophisticated technology and knowhow. Something bright and breezy was needed to appeal to as many as possible.

It was the 'Everyman' dream of so many companies of the past. The dream that there was a vast untapped market for two-wheeled transport. Motorcycles had so many advantages for so many people. They could thread through traffic, were easy to park, light on fuel, cheap to buy and run. If only . . . if only they were quieter, cleaner, lighter, easier to use and gave some protection from the weather.

There had been attempts in the past to break into this market. Pre-war, the machines were usually too heavy and slow, for either they used a minute engine or hung enclosure on a sluggish, touring model which reduced its performance even further and increased the risk of a hernia when parking. Postwar there were mopeds of limited performance and the scooter boom. The latter very nearly did the trick, for it offered many of the advantages with few of the problems. In the West on paved roads thousands turned to it before more money and the mods and rockers cults made them favour four wheels.

Away from tarmac roads the scooter with its inherent small wheels was less successful. Dirt roads and potholes highlighted the difficulties of

traction and suspension, while in many countries the size and sophistication was too expensive for the bulk of the population. And yet it was so nearly what was wanted thought Honda and from that was born the most successful two-wheeler of all time—the Super Cub.

The format of the new machine was completely new as was the concept for the mechanics. For far too long the aim had been to produce a cheap machine and the result was always the same. Mediocre performance, poor reliability, dreadful electrics, doubtful starting and dissatisfied riders. Honda decided that from the start his machines, and the Super Cub in particular, would be inexpensive, not cheap, and achieve this by the use of the best of mass-production techniques. Parts would be die-cast in aluminium to leave the minimum of machining, moulded in plastic to remove the need to paint, stamped out in sheet for easy machine welding. Most of all, the electrics would be built in, properly designed and made to survive their environment. Connectors would connect and continue to do their job for years, to part when required to and rejoin as the customer had often wished for but had never been granted.

The Super Cub was a combination of the developed and sophisticated moped popular in Europe and the traditional scooter. It became known as a scooterette or step-thru and in a few years these were generic terms within the motorcycle industry. The machine fulfilled the aims for Mr (and Mrs and Miss) Everyone, for it was light, adequately nippy, easy to ride, easy to clean and had its mechanics decently clad and out of sight. It had full-sized wheels (like a bicycle thought the many), a comfortable seat and was fully equipped for commuter travel.

The Super Cub was absolutely right from the word go and the sales were enormous. It became, in its various forms, the Model T Ford of the two-wheeled world and on 7 April, 1983, the 15 millionth model was built. It was a phenomenon and even after a quarter of a cen-

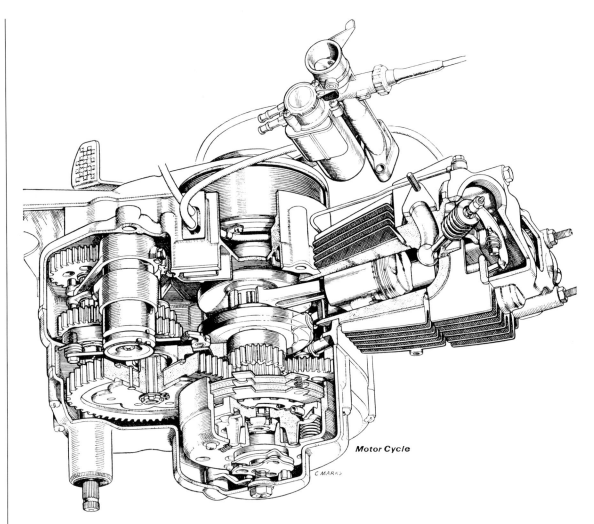

Motor Cycle

C MARKS

tury the sales showed little signs of abating, having run consistently at over half a million per annum for most years from 1960 on. 1963 was the best year of all at 889,005, but even 1973, the worst at 469,732, was hardly poor business.

In all that time the Super Cub changed in detail but not in concept or even much in appearance. The latest model is so obviously related to the first it is hard to realize the span of years between them or not to appreciate the brilliance of the original design. If ever a machine mobilized the people and gave them transport

it was the tiny Super Cub. It truly sold worldwide.

The first model was launched in August 1958 as the C100 and set the style and layout from then on. The step-through feature came from a frame that ran down low between headstock and seat but not flat enough to resemble a scooter, for the engine unit was installed beneath this area. This allowed the use of full-sized wheels, kept the weight distribution right and made for a slim profile for easy traffic negotiation.

The engine unit had a single cylinder laid nearly horizontal with dimensions of 40 × 39 mm

Above **Honda at Earls Court in 1964 with Masako Buroton on a C100**

Above left **Line drawing of the C100 engine of 50 cc with ohv and three-speed gearbox**

Right **The C102 in 1961 with electric starter mounted above crankcase**

and a capacity of 49 cc. Compression ratio was 8·5:1 and on this it produced 4·5 bhp at 9500 rpm, both figures well above the norm for the period. The crankshaft was a pressed assembly which ran in a pair of ball races with the mainshafts integral with the flywheels. The big end bearing used caged rollers and these ran directly on the plain crankpin, pressed into each web, and the connecting rod eye.

The gudgeon pin ran directly in the rod and supported a conventional piston with three rings, including the oil control one. The cylinder was cast in iron with the fins running along its length to suit the installation and was mounted on four long studs screwed into the crankcase. The cast-

ing extended as needed to encompass the two pushrods and to provide an oil drain from the cylinder head.

The head was also cast in iron with a well in the top for the valves, a flange on top for the carburettor and a hole and two studs beneath to take the exhaust pipe. The sparking plug went in at an angle on the left. Sealing between head and barrel was achieved by a spigot up into the head with a circular copper gasket above it.

Nuts on the four long studs held both head and barrel in place and a further four bolts attached the light alloy rocker box to the head. Each rocker oscillated on its own spindle, held in place by an outer cap, with a compression spring and thrust washer to take up end play. Screw adjusters in the outer rocker ends enabled the valve gaps to be set and access to these was via a pair of caps with large hexagons for a spanner. The rocker cap was to become a Honda feature on many models.

The valves themselves were held shut by duplex springs retained by a collar and split collets. They were opened by a camshaft which ran directly in the crankcase and was driven by a spur gear pair from the right end of the crankshaft. The cam gear was held on the end of the camshaft by a single bolt and located to it by a pin. Forward of the cams went flat feet tappets and pushrods transmitted the cam form to the rockers. It was the barest minimum of parts for an overhead-valve engine.

The crankcase was split on the vertical centre line and die cast in light alloy. Incorporated within it was the three-speed gearbox with its positive stop change mechanism controlled by a pedal on the left which was driven by an automatic clutch housed under a cover on the right. To the left, on the end of the crankshaft, went a flywheel magneto with the contact points mounted on the stator plate. An additional small cover gave access to them for adjustment and the rotor incorporated a centrifugal advance mechanism.

CZ100 Monkey bike in 1961, a mini in front of a Mini

Above **The Sports Cub C110 built from 1960 and as the C111 with single seat**

Right **The C114 in 1963 with low-level exhaust but otherwise as the C110. Also known as the C110D**

Left The C240 Port-Cub in 1963, two speeds and modified frame

Below The 87 cc ohv C200 built from 1963 in sports format with leading link forks

Below right Sports CS90 with ohc engine on show at Earls Court in late 1964

Also on the left was the final drive sprocket under a cover and this was locked to the gearbox output shaft by a method to be repeated on many more models. The shaft was splined as usual, but in place of the normal threaded end it was cut off and a single groove machined in it just outboard of the sprocket position. The sprocket was splined and had two tapped holes in it. A small plate was also splined and had two holes to match those in the sprocket. The trick was that the plate fitted to the splines reached the groove and was rotated to be out of step with the splines. In this position it could not come off and only when it was so placed would the small bolts attach it to the sprocket.

Simple, elegant, cheap and easy to work with.

The lubrication system was also simple, for it dispensed with an oil pump. The oil was common to both engine and gearbox and contained in the base of the crankcase. Most of the parts relied on splash for their supply, but the big end went a little better and used an early and once common scheme. This was the rod dip and for this the connecting rod was forged with a small extension below the big end eye. As the crankshaft turned the rod extension dipped beneath the level of the oil, which was thus forced through a small drilled hole on to the big end rollers — quite effective provided the oil level was maintained and the engine loads were not too high.

To lubricate the rocker box, the camshaft,

which lay in the sump and was thus well supplied with oil, was machined with a spiral groove at one end, the action of which pumped the oil into an external pipe which ran to the top of the rocker box. Engine breathing was done with a labyrinth passage cast into the upper crankcase wall with an external pipe to take any gases away.

The carburettor was a simple slide type which bolted directly to the cylinder head so as to act in a downdraught manner. Built into it was a flap choke controlled by a small lever and the top of the float chamber incorporated a three-position tap giving off, on and reserve positions. It also incorporated a filter.

The carburettor was connected by hose to an air cleaner mounted on the frame and the exhaust pipe attached by a flange and two studs. The silencer went low down on the right.

The clutch went on the right end of the crank-shaft outboard of the timing pinion and the primary drive gear. This latter meshed with a larger gear splined to the gearbox input shaft and retained on it by circlips.

The jobs the clutch was called upon to do made it quite an assembly, complex in operation but simple to put together. In the first place it had to take up the drive as the engine speed increased, and did this with weights that moved out under the influence of centrifugal force. Thus

a gear could be selected and the throttle opened, when the clutch would engage and the machine moved off without stalling. End of novice's greatest fear and problem.

The drive was taken through plain and friction plates of normal form and the outer ones were lightly spring loaded apart to ensure good separation when needed. Firmer springs clamped them together when under the driving load.

The clutch centre, splined to the driven plates, was not directly attached to the primary drive gear but was positioned on a part of that gear machined into a quick start thread. The effect of this was twofold. First it allowed use of the kickstart pedal to lock up the clutch and thus turn the engine over, and second it did a similar thing on the overrun.

There was one further embellishment to the clutch and this was a ball-and-ramp lifting mechanism mounted outboard of it in the outer cover. Cunningly this was linked to the gear pedal so that, regardless of which way that was moved, the clutch plates were separated and gear changing made easy.

It was possible in theory to upset the design by riding with the left foot on the gear pedal thus holding the clutch partly disengaged, but in practice this failed to be a problem. A bonus of the design was that the machine could be push started if necessary, something not always possible with automatics.

The gearbox itself was of conventional all-indirect, cross-over design with the three speeds selected by a sliding gear on the input and sliding dog on the output shafts. The two selectors rode on a barrel cam and this had pins in one end for the positive stop mechanism to engage with.

The engine unit was held in the frame by two bolts, one at the top of the crankcase and the other at the rear. The frame was elegantly simple and built up from tube and pressings together. At the front the headstock was braced to a tube that ran back to a point above the crankcase.

Above **The CD90 with the telescopic forks fitted from 1968. More of a touring model**

Top **The 1965 CM90 with ohv engine and three speeds**

Left **The S65 sports machine with ohc engine and much as the 50 and 90 cc models**

The C320 on show in 1966. Ohv engine, four speeds and T-bone frame

There it was welded to an assembly of pressings and these went up and back to form the main spine and then the rear mudguard. The centre area was also taken down behind the engine to support it as well as the rear fork pivot and the centre stand.

The interior of the frame was also pressed into service, with the front end acting as a connection between the air filter and the carburettor hose. In the centre the space was used to house the electrics and tools with a plastic cover on each side held by a turn screw.

The centre stand was firm and easy to use and its pivot tube was shared by the rear brake pedal, which went on the right. The footrests were not attached to the frame at all but bolted directly to the underside of the crankcase. In that position they were also used to carry the engine unit about. When the time came to carry a passenger

the footrests for them were bolted straight on to the pivoted fork, which was built up from pressings and controlled by a pair of spring units. On its left arm it carried a full chaincase that kept nearly all the dirt at bay even if it was not sealed.

At the front of the frame went leading link forks. These had pressed steel blades and short, forged links pivoted on bushes. Further bushes connected the links to the spring units, which

Left **The Honda in a wheel, a 1967 P50**

Below **The C90 step-thru in 1968, one of the very many**

Above **1967 CL90, a sports model with some trail bike pretensions**

Above **Monkey bike Z50 for 1969 with many changes but original concept**

Below **SS50 in 1968, the small sports model**

were concealed within the fork legs. A truly enormous, moulded plastic mudguard was fitted, which was light, rustproof and efficient.

Both wheels had full-width, light alloy hubs with single leading shoe drum brakes. The front hub drove the speedometer and the rear was itself driven by a sprocket carrier via shock absorber rubbers. The wheel rims were steel and held to the hubs by wire spokes, while both tyres were the same size at 2·25 × 17 in.

The petrol tank was mounted on top of the frame with the two fuel lines for main and reserve supplies carried out of sight within the frame. The tank was styled into the general lines of the machine and carried the single seat on its top surface which hinged up to give access to the filler cap. Behind the seat, mounted on the frame, went a carrier.

The form of the scooterette came from its combined apron and legshields. This was a one-piece plastic moulding which dropped over the frame tube to enclose the engine top half and which ran forwards and then outwards to form the shields. These were taken up to the top of the headstock and on the way fitted around the air cleaner.

The apron colour was matched by the side covers and behind one of these went the battery, rectifier, fuse and winker relay. The electrics were very complete and well thought out for such a basic model and this proved to be one of its strong points. Turn indicators were fitted to the handlebar pressing at the front and the frame at the rear. The ignition switch went under the left side cover to allow easy connection to the items related to it. Thumb switches built into each handlebar controlled headlight, winkers and horn, the last item being mounted in the fork assembly just below the headlamp. The speedometer went into the centre of the handlebar pressing, which in turn carried one mirror with a second hole ready for an optional matching one. The pressing concealed the brake and electric cables, while the twistgrip was of the slide

type so that the cable could also be easily hidden.

This then was the first of the many millions destined to mobilize the world on to two wheels. The sales figures were enormous from day one and from August to December 1958 some 24,000 were built. In time the production became so organized that a Honda 50 rolled off the line every 12 seconds. The Super Cub proved totally fuss free and able to withstand the abuse and ignorance of the less developed countries. It ran along at just over 40 mph, so its performance was quite adequate for the cities of the West and the trails of the East. In doing all this it gave Honda a firm base to build on and the money to investigate all manner of exciting machines.

Honda had to go out into the world to sell the Super Cub, plus the rest of the range, and began this in 1959, when American Honda was established. This was followed by Honda Deutschland in 1961, Honda Benelux and Honda in England in 1962, Honda France in 1964 and the company title, Honda UK, was adopted in 1965. Often this formalization followed an interim period when machines were imported by smaller concerns, and Hondas were shown in Europe as early as 1959.

The sixties were a period when the English industry began its decline on to hard times. It

The CT90 or how to make a step-thru into a trail bike

had coasted through the fifties on its earlier success and dominance and left innovation to the Germans and Italians. It went on to enjoy good sales in the sixties in the USA, but these were not of its own making; they came from the work put in by Honda in the main plus the other three major Japanese firms. By the end of the decade the Japanese had moved into the traditional

Left **1971 C70 with parking light in headstock not used by other models**

Below **An ST70 on test late in 1972. Fold-up concept but larger than the Monkey bike**

English big bike field and, suffering from management thrombosis, the English industry died in commercial terms. A few flickers of life kept the embers warm, but production was minimal by the eighties.

Honda began their export drive in the USA and set out from the start to expand the total market. They side-stepped the traditional motorcycle world with its leather jacket and down-market image by advertising in a whole range of cosmopolitan journals. They devised their most famous theme 'You meet the nicest people on a Honda' and plugged it in the colleges, placing advertisement copy in general magazines such as *Reader's Digest*, *Time* and *Life*, magazines for men and women, and without missing the motorcycle specialists added some to the car journals.

The advertising worked. It increased the market size tenfold, which also helped Honda's competitors, but most of all it brought sales volume to pay for up-market presentation and respectability. Motorcycling became an accepted way to go to the office, go shopping, nip over to the golf club or just to get out and have fun. As the market grew so Honda began to narrow the focus of their adverts. From selling motorcycling itself they moved to specific aspects and sections of their range and finally to individual models.

The advertising worked. To many laymen motorcycle meant Honda, much to the chagrin of Kawasaki, Suzuki, Triumph and Yamaha. The ads and the TV jingles all persuaded thousands to avoid the traffic jams, cut costs and enjoy the ride. And at the forefront of it all was the C100.

In 1960 it was joined by the C102, which was the same model with the addition of electric starting and a change to coil ignition. The starter was a small direct current motor bolted to the top of the crankcase and it drove the crankshaft by chain. A one-way roller clutch was built into the driven sprocket and this went behind the alternator rotor. A retaining plate prevented it from moving out and the chain itself kept the small driving sprocket in place on the splines on the motor shaft. No other fixing was provided or needed. With this addition to easy starting the scooterette became even more attractive to lady riders.

Also introduced in 1960 was the type Z or CZ100, better known as the Monkey bike. This used the C100 engine unit in the smallest possible configuration for road use. A rigid tubular frame was fitted with rigid forks styled to suggest telescopics or leading links. Tiny fat tyres of 3·50 × 5 in. section were fitted, a single seat, and the whole machine could be carried in a car boot.

The Z was only meant for very short-distance travel and for paddock use, but the novelty brought its own publicity as personalities around the world were pictured using them. Honda painted the frame and forks scarlet, and finished the tank with chrome plating, so the Monkey bike was easily noticed even if it was so small.

While the Z was fun and the step-thru just the job for commuting, the youth of Japan wanted something a little more sporty, so Honda obliged with the C110. This was a pure motorcycle which used a suitably modified C100 engine unit. Extra power came from a raised

PC50 in 1975, one of many basic mopeds built by Honda

compression ratio and to deal with the added heat the cylinder head material was changed to light alloy. At first the three speeds were retained but were soon changed for four, in both cases controlled by a rocking gear pedal and a manual clutch.

A spine frame with pivoted fork rear suspension was used and the inlet tract ran back from the head to a distant carburettor. This breathed from an air cleaner located within the frame. The exhaust ran up on the right to a raised silencer fitted with a perforated, chrome-plated heat

The SL90 trail model from 1969, a machine more off-road than the CL90

shield. The front forks were leading links on the lines of the C100 and side covers to enclose the electrics were fitted along with full equipment and a dualseat.

The same model was also available as the C111, fitted with a single seat, and the C110D or C114 with low-level exhaust. In all cases the rear chain was fully enclosed, the tank humped in style and the rear mudguard fitted with a small flat tail to keep wheel spray at bay.

For riders who sought a touch more capacity Honda introduced the C105 step-thru and C115 sports in 1961. Both copied the 50 cc models, but were fitted with an engine bored out to 42 mm and 54 cc. Otherwise they were the same machines as the C100 and C110. Two years later a further version of the C105 was built for use

in a more off-road situation. To this end the tyres were changed for ones with more of a competition pattern tread, pannier frames were added to both sides of the rear carrier, a front carrier bag frame went on to the forks and a supplementary fuel tank was fitted in front of the standard one on top of the apron panel. All these changes enabled the machine to be used for greater distances away from the highway and to carry more bulky loads.

Before that, in 1962, a further version of the C100 appeared as the Port-Cub C240. This was little changed, but had the apron cut away to expose the complete engine unit, while the frame was altered to run the spine forward to the headstock.

In England Honda decided to attempt to win the prestigious Maudes Trophy. This had been donated to the ACU by George Pettyt of Maudes Motor Mart, Exeter, to be awarded annually to the firm whose machines completed the best certified test of the year. The tests had to show reliability and economy rather than speed, and the award, originally known as the Pettyt Cup, was only made if the tests were of an acceptable standard.

The trophy was first won by Norton for the years 1923 to 1926 and then went to various English firms up to 1939, when Triumph took it.

The very popular CB125S built from 1970–78. This is a 1973 version

After the war it was rather forgotten until BSA won it in 1952, after which interest lapsed again. Honda decided to publicize the 50 in Britain by running a C100, a C102 and a C114 round Goodwood racing circuit for seven days and if successful to claim the trophy. A 20-strong team of riders was assembled and in late October the three machines set off. The weather was cold and it rained every day, but all three machines completed the week running well, so the Trophy went to Honda, where it stayed until 1973, when BMW took it only to lose it to Suzuki a year later.

1963 brought a new sports model to the Honda range to meet a swing in Japan from 50 cc to 80 cc. A mere 30 cc may not seem much, but for the young rider it was a big increase on his existing model with its moped-style capacity. Suddenly there was an 80 cc class in Japan, created more by Suzuki than anyone.

The Honda answer was the C200, which was on the same lines as the C110 but with a larger engine. The bore and stroke were both increased to dimensions of 49 × 46 mm, which gave a capacity of 86·7 cc. Compression ratio was 8·0:1 and the power output 6·5 bhp at 8000 rpm.

There were detail changes to the engine with the rocker box being held down with the head and barrel on four studs, but the major alteration was the adoption of an oil pump and pressure oil feed. The pump was located in the crankcase and driven by the end of the camshaft. The oil was pumped into the crankshaft via the right cover and the clutch body, the two being sealed with seals and O-rings. The body was also used to filter the oil by providing a chamber into which any debris could centrifuge while the oil was taken along the crankshaft and chamber centre axis, a feature also used in many other Honda models. Oil was also pumped to the rocker box.

The remainder of the machine was taken from the C110 with manual clutch, four-speed gearbox, spine frame, leading link forks and drum brakes. The tyre section was increased slightly and the rear mudguard spray flap was not fitted,

but otherwise equipment was full and included turn indicators and a mirror.

In 1964 another sports 90 appeared and while at first sight it appeared to be much as the C200 it incorporated several important new steps for the small Honda models. These were an overhead camshaft, telescopic forks, bigger wheels and a revised form of the spine frame. Not that ohc was new to Honda, for the SA single had used it as far back as 1955, but the CS90, as the new model was properly called (shortened to S90 in the UK, at least), was the first single so equipped to be seen outside Japan in quantity.

The engine dimensions were changed from those of the C200 to 50 × 45·6 mm, which made

Left One of the All Terrain Cycles, the ATC110, and great fun to drive on any off-road surface

Left below Another moped, the PF50 Graduate in 1973 with rigid frame

Right Another miniature, the QA50 in 1974 with rigid frame and telescopic forks

Below A press-man trying hard on a Chaly CF70 in 1975

Above **Very popular trail bike, the XL250 in 1973, later fitted with twin exhaust pipes**

Right **Competition two-stroke, the 1973 CR250M built for motocross and called Elsinore, at least in the USA**

Above **1976 version of the XL250, not much changed from its launch and good at its job**

Left **The smaller motocross model, the CR125M in 1974**

Left **Enduro models in Australia, the MT250 and MT125 (right), based on the CR series**

Below **The Bials, or bike and trials, model at Tokyo in 1972. Typed the TL125, it used the SL125 engine**

the capacity 89·5 cc. The compression ratio was 8·2:1 and the power 8 bhp at 9500 rpm. Engine construction was to set the pattern for the small Hondas for many years, with the camshaft drive by chain on the left and many features taken from the earlier models.

The camshaft ran directly in the cylinder head and the left bearing was formed with two cut-outs to enable the cams to pass through it on assembly. The rockers pivoted on pins set in holes and retained adjusters at their outer ends. Access to these continued to be via caps. The rocker pins were prevented from coming out once the engine was assembled by the four long holding-down studs passing either side of them. The studs' holes also acted as oil pipes to pass the lubricant to the cylinder head.

Both head and barrel were cast in light alloy, the first with an iron skull to provide the valve seats and plug thread. The cam chain passage was formed in both on the left and further covers sealed the top and two sides of the cambox. The left cover also provided a mounting for the coil ignition contact points, whose cam was driven by the camshaft via an auto-advance mechanism.

The cam chain was driven by a sprocket pressed on to the crankshaft and linked to another which was bolted to the camshaft with three screws. These were pitched to fix in only one position and timing marks on the cylinder centreline made valve timing simple to set. A guide roller ran freely on a pin within the cylinder tunnel with the chain running either side of it, and near the crankshaft went a tensioner sprocket and a spring-loaded jockey wheel. The latter kept the chain in tension with a spring plunger to apply the load, but the sprocket had another job. Its spindle ran across the engine to the oil pump, which it drove via a dog connection.

The remainder of the engine unit was essentially as the C200 with manual clutch and four-speed gearbox. The spine frame was formed in

Above **Honda Dax or ST90 for 1973, one of a series of models**

Top **The XR75 four-stroke motocross model for youngsters**

the manner of a letter T, so that although it supported the seat in the usual way the rear mudguard was separate. Telescopic front forks replaced the leading links and the tyre size was increased to 2·50 × 18 in.

The idea of an overhead camshaft and the brilliantly simple engine construction were too good to be kept for one model only, so in 1965 two more appeared as the CS50 and CS65. The engines followed the same pattern with the smaller based on dimensions of 39 × 41·4 mm and the larger bored out a little to 44 mm and 63 cc. Ignition was by flywheel magneto mounted on the left crankshaft end, so the cambox was finished with a round cover on that side. The frame details remained as for the C110 with leading link front forks, 17 in. wheels and the rear mudguard formed as part of the frame. Exhaust pipes remained upswept to a silencer with stylish heat shield.

The 63 cc engine was also fitted to the step-thru to create the C65 and in this guise it was fitted with a camshaft, with softer timing, the three-speed gearbox and the automatic clutch. It also gained a pillion seat on the rear carrier with footrests in the sides of the pivoted fork.

In other respects the machine was as the C100.

With yet another rearrangement of the parts at his disposal, Mr Honda also produced the step-thru CM90 using the C200 engine with three-speed gearbox and automatic clutch in the C65 cycle parts, and just to confuse the customers added the CD90 with the CS90 engine in the C200 cycle parts with leading link forks to produce a touring version of the sports model. It could carry two, but the pillion pad was attached to a carrier so that it could be replaced by luggage. In addition the engine was detuned a little by half a horsepower and 500 revs.

1966 brought what many consider to be the best known of the Honda step-thru family, the

C50. This used the engine from the CS50 with the transmission usual to the scooterette and was to be built for year after year after year. For this engine, and the C65, the cylinder was cast in iron, while the head was in light alloy. The construction was so simple that servicing could be easily carried out anywhere around the globe. The whole machine was equally easy and the C50 ran from Alaska to Zanzibar without a murmur.

For the sports rider came the C320 with the C110 engine in the T-bone frame and telescopic forks of the CS90. This was in fact a moped and thus it had a restricted power output and was fitted with pedals, but otherwise looked the works. Japanese youth loved them.

A very different form of moped was the P25, which was also known as the little Honda and given the type number P50 in many countries. It was unique as it had the entire engine unit built into the rear wheel assembly and thus resembled the F-type Cub of 1952.

The engine retained the overhead camshaft but changed its dimensions to 42 × 35·6 mm. Compression ratio was 9:1, but the power was restricted to 1·2 bhp at 4200 rpm with maximum torque at a low 2500 rpm. An automatic clutch connected the engine to the wheel via three sets of chains and sprockets to get the desired reduction ratio. Ignition was by flywheel magneto and the lighting direct.

The engine was hung low down on the left of the wheel, which went into a pressed steel frame fitted with leading link forks. No rear suspension was provided, but a good saddle was fitted and with the pedals the machine looked much like a bicycle. The fuel tank formed a rear carrier and both brakes were hand operated, the front a small drum but the rear an external contracting device.

Normally the wheel size was 17 in., but some machines were built in Europe and known as the Dutch P50. All these had 19 in. rims and all models had a 2·00 in. front and 2·25 in. rear tyre section.

In the 90 cc class there was a further change to the step-thru with the adoption of the camshaft engine. This first produced the CM91, which used the CM90 frame, and then the C90, which joined the C50 to run on into the eighties. A further version of the CS90 came on the scene, fitted with a single seat and rear carrier in place of a dualseat, but otherwise it was the same sports motorcycle with T-spine frame.

New in the street scrambler mould was the CL90, which followed the lines set down by earlier twin-cylinder Hondas aimed at the American market. For this they were modified to a degree for off-road use but retained such road model features as a close-fitting front mudguard. The exhaust system would be upswept and fitted with a chrome-plated heat shield, the rear mudguard shortened and the rear lamp moved round it closer to the seat and more out of harm's way, the tyre type changed for improved off-road grip and the gearing maybe lowered.

Such machines preceded the later trail models and were of limited use away from the highway, but this did not stop many enjoying them. They could cope well enough with dry earth tracks while offering a good road performance, so sold well to riders who wanted some mild adventure at weekends or a machine more suited to reaching a choice backwoods, fishing or camping spot.

Because large street scramblers became popular as a class, riders of small models came to want something that looked similar, hence the development of the CL90. This was based firmly on the CS90 with the camshaft engine, T-spine frame and telescopic forks. In addition to the raised exhaust and tyre changes it also featured high and wide bars.

1967 brought further variations on this theme and others in the 50 cc class. New was the CL50, looking just like the 90 and fitted with the four-speed camshaft engine also used by the CD50, which kept to the cycle parts of the CS50 and thus had leading link forks and the older form of spine frame.

New and more sporting was the SS50, which used the same engine but with the power output raised to 6 bhp at 11,000 rpm. It was coupled to a gearbox containing five speeds and the unit went into the T-spine frame fitted with telescopic forks. A nicely styled tank was set off by a dualseat with racing lines and a raised exhaust was fitted.

A new version of the Monkey bike appeared typed the Z50M or CZ50 and fitted with a modified form of the C50 engine. This was detuned down to 2·5 bhp at 6000 rpm and retained the three-speed gearbox. The frame continued tubular and rigid, as were the forks, which were just tubes flattened at their lower ends to take the wheel. Tyre size was 4·00 × 5 in. and both the seat and handlebars folded down for stowage. It made a worthy replacement.

The C50 step-thru was joined by the C50M, with electric starting courtesy of a small direct current motor and a chain, as on the C102, and the C65M emerged in the same way. In both cases the change brought coil ignition.

The final new model for 1967 was the CT90, which is best described as a trail version of the C90. To achieve this the plastic apron was removed, a crash bar run on each side of the machine from the headstock to under the engine unit, a very raised exhaust was fitted and finally competition tyres and cut-down mudguards. The result was odd in appearance but practical in use.

For 1968 there was a smaller version, the CT50, available and two more machines using the 65 cc engine. The CT50 copied the lines of the 90 but with a neat cover over the exposed frame tube to give it some style. Like the 90 it had a dual-range three-speed gearbox to give a total of six gears to cover both on- and off-road situations.

The 65 cc machines were the CL65 in street scrambler form with telescopic forks, T-spine frame and upswept exhaust and the CD65. This used the same frame, but the forks were fitted with shrouds rather than gaiters and a separate seat and pillion pad plus the touring mudguards gave it a touring model line. That year also saw the CD50 with the T-spine frame, telescopic front forks and a single seat, so in all its appearance was a good deal changed from its first version. Also the CD90 changed to telescopics and the SS50 appeared with the low-level exhaust of the CD50.

1969 brought a new capacity, two new model styles and a new moped. The new capacity was

Engine unit of the larger trials model, the TL250 in 1975

70 cc and was achieved by boring the 50 cc camshaft engine out to 47 mm and 71·8 cc. The engine went into the step-thru to give the C70 and this joined the 50 cc and 90 cc models to run on for many years.

The engine was also used in the ST70, which was a new form of machine for Honda. Other companies called them fun bikes and they were miniature machines, smaller than the normal motorcycle but larger than the Monkey type.

Honda gave them the name DAX and produced a smaller 50 cc version as well, the ST50. Both machines used the step-thru camshaft engine with three-speed gearbox and ran on fat 3·50 × 10 in. tyres. The frames were of the spine type with the seat on top and the fuel tank and battery inside the frame beneath it. Front suspension was by telescopic forks and both upswept and low exhaust systems were used at various times on either model. For town use they were good and they folded up easily for stowage and carrying.

The new moped for 1969 was the PC50 and at first this was fitted with the camshaft engine,

SL125

Technical Specification

Engine Unit

Type: Air Cooled 4-stroke Engine chain driven O.H.C.
Cylinder Arrangement: Single cylinder 15° inclined from vertical
Bore & Stroke: 56 × 49.5 mm 2.204 × 1.949 ins)
Compression Ratio: 9.5:1
Cylinder Capacity: 122 cc (7.44 cu ins)
Carburettor: Keihin piston valve type Venturi dia 22 mm
Ignition: Battery & Ignition Coil
Oil Capacity: 1.0 litre (1.0.22 Imp. gall s)
Starting System: Kickstarter
Spark Plug: NGK D8ES
Clutch: Wet Multi-Plate
Generator: AC 0.045 KW 10,000 R.P.M.
Battery: 6 Volt 6 A.H.
Air Filtration: Oiled Polyurethane Foam
Transmission: 5-speed constant mesh type
Primary Reduction: 4.055
Gear Ratios: 1st 2.769 2nd 1.722 3rd 1.272 4th 1.043 5th 0.84
Final Reduction: 3.266 (Drive Sprocket 15T Driven Sprocket 49T)
Maximum Power: 12 P.S. 9,000 R.P.M.
Maximum Torque: 1.0 kg m 8,000 R.P.M.

Frame

Type: Double cradle
Front Suspension: Telescopic fork Travel 141 mm
Rear Suspension: Swinging Arm travel 83 mm
Tyres: Front 2.75 - 21 4PR Semi Knobbly Rear 3.25 - 18 4PR Semi Knobbly
Tyre Pressures: Front 1.8 Kg/cm (26 p.s.i.) Rear 2.0 Kg/cm (28.5 p.s.i.)
Brakes: Front Internal Expanding Type Lining Swept area 86.4 cm (13.4 sq.ins)
Rear Internal Expanding Type Lining Swept area 86.4 cm (13.4 sq.ins)
Petrol Tank: 7.0 litres (1.5 Imp.gal. Res 1.5 litres (0.3 Imp.gal)
Overall Length: 1970 mm (77.5 ins)
Overall Width: 810 mm (31.8 ins)
Overall Height: 1110 mm (43.7 ins)
Wheelbase: 1265 mm (49.8 ins)
Seating Height: 811 mm (11.8 ins)
Ground Clearance: 215 mm (8.4 ins)
Footrest Height: 290 mm (11.4 ins)
Dry Weight: 95 Kg (209.38 lbs)
Curb Weight: 102 Kg (224.80 lbs)
Turning Circle: 3.8 m (12.46 ft)

but this was later changed to a pushrod type. This engine had the 42 × 35·6 mm dimensions of the P25 and was similar in layout to the old C100. The valve gear was truly simple, with the camshaft and its drive sprocket die-cast in light alloy and run direct in the crankcase. Its end drove the oil pump which served the rocker box, while the big end relied on a scoop on the connecting rod dipping into the oil surface as on the older

engine. It was a neat if small machine.

An automatic clutch drove a reduction gear from which a chain connected to the rear wheel. Built into the unit was a cross-shaft carrying the pedals and this drove to the gears by a small internal chain. Ignition was by flywheel magneto and the exhaust went low down on the right.

The frame was a simple beam built up from pressings, so the controls and wiring could be

XL125-K3

Technical Specifications

Engine Unit

Type: Air Cooled, Single Cylinder, 4 Stroke, Chain Driven Overhead Camshaft
Bore & Stroke: 56·5 mm × 49·5 mm (2·224 × 1·949 ins)
Total Capacity: 124 cc (7·6 cu ins)
Compression Ratio: 9·4:1
Carburettor: Piston Valve Type
Ignition: Magneto
Lubrication System: Wet Sump, Forced Feed
Alternator: AC Generator 0·064 kw. a 5000 R.P.M.
Battery: 6 Volt 4 A.H.
Starting Method: Kickstarter
Spark Plug: NGK D 8ES L, ND X24ES
Clutch: Wet Multiplate
Transmission: 5-speed constant mesh
Primary Reduction: 4·055
Gear Ratios: 1st 2·769, 2nd 1·722, 3rd 1·272, 4th 1·000, 5th 0·814
Final Reduction: 3·466, Drive Sprocket 15T, Driven 52T
Maximum Power: 12·5 (P.S.)
Fuel Required: 2 Star Minimum

Frame

Type: Semi Double Cradle
Front Suspension: Telescopic, Fork Offset Axle
Travel 165 mm (6·5 ins)
Rear Suspension: Swinging Arm,
Travel 93 mm (3·7 ins)
Tyres: Front 2·75 × 21, Rear 3·50 × 18
Tyre Pressures: Front - Rear 1·5 kg/cm² (21 p.s.i.)
Brakes: Front - Rear Internal Expanding Shoe
Overall Length: 2060 mm (81·1 ins)
Overall Width: 830 mm (32·7 ins)
Overall Height: 1105 mm (43·5 ins)
Wheelbase: 1315 mm (51·8 ins)
Ground Clearance: 215 mm (8·5 ins)
Seat Height: 815 mm (32·1 ins)
Dry Weight: 99 kg (218 lbs)

hidden from sight within it. The fuel tank was tucked on to the left side under the saddle and was matched by a tool box on the right. Pivoted fork rear and leading link front suspension was provided and the wheels had 19 in. rims and full-width, light alloy hubs with drum brakes.

The second new model style was represented by the SL90, which was a step further off road than the CL model. It was far nearer to being a trail bike and was a good deal changed from the earlier machines with their road frames. The engine remained the 90 cc camshaft unit with four-speed gearbox, but the chassis was all new.

The frame was a duplex cradle tubular one which gave the engine far more support and protection. The forks lost their gaiters and close-fitting front mudguard while the seat and rear guard were kept short for off-road use. A high-level exhaust was fitted and a deep, narrow fuel tank.

The CS90 and CL90 both continued to offer sports and street scrambler forms, while the touring CD90 continued with its telescopic forks, leading links now generally being used only for the step-thru models and mopeds.

1970 brought a new decade and more new Honda models. The Monkey bike gained telescopic front forks and 3·50 × 8 in. tyres, but its seat no longer folded down. In some versions it was given a new tank badge carrying a new name 'Mini-Trail'. New machines using the 70 cc camshaft engine were the street scrambler CL70 and the touring CD70, both of which used the T-spine frame fitted with telescopic forks. The tourer had thinner tyres but bigger mudguards.

In the 90 cc class both the SL and CL models received very major changes, in effect becoming new machines, and were joined by a sports road version, the CB90. All three used a new engine with the cylinder set near the vertical and only inclined forward a few degrees. Inside, the single overhead camshaft was still chain driven on the left with an automatic tensioner just inboard of the generator. The CL gearbox contained four speeds, but the other two both had five. However, their engines differed in performance, although all three shared dimensions of 48 × 49·5 mm, a capacity of 89·6 cc and a compression ratio of 9·5:1. The CB90 power was 10·5 bhp at 10,500 rpm, while the other two were lower at 9000 and 9500.

These new engine units went into frames built up from tubes in diamond form with a main pressing to support the pivoted fork and others to act as braces. Telescopic forks were fitted with exposed stanchions for the SL, gaiters for the CL and shrouds for the CB. Wheels and tyres also varied to suit the purpose and the exhausts were tailored up or down to suit.

Having laid out a new engine design Honda decided to use it to the full and with the CB90 came the slightly larger CB100 plus the greater

CB125S. Both repeated the vertical engine and reached their 99·1 cc and 121·9 cc capacities by being bored out to 50·5 and 56 mm respectively, while keeping to the 49·5 mm stroke. Compression ratios were both 9·5:1 and power outputs 11·5 and 12 bhp. Five-speed gearboxes were used and the cycle parts were as the 90.

To round matters off the 125 engine was also used for a touring CD125S, which had to manage with four speeds, and the trail SL125S, which had five. In other respects they mirrored the 90 cc models.

Completely new was the US90, which later became better known as the All Terrain Cycle or ATC in a variety of sizes. These machines had three very fat, very soft balloon tyres set in tricycle pattern and these alone provided the suspension. With these tyres they could run on just about any off-road surface, including sand, mud, snow, grass and even in very deep water.

They were to prove very practical for outdoor work and tremendous fun to ride. With the stability of three wheels the average rider went quicker over rough ground and if needed he could carry a great deal of equipment or goods. It was possible to upend them, but even if the front shot skywards the rider was gently laid to earth on his back and only had to remember to kick the machine forward and away from him.

The US90 used the camshaft engine with four-speed gearbox hung from a spine frame. This carried the simple unsprung front fork at one end and the rigid rear axle at the other. There was no differential fitted, so steering response was poor until the rider learned to let the inner wheel lift when he wanted to turn, a technique that took about five minutes to learn. Both brakes went on the rear wheel, the clutch was automatic, the throttle a spring-loaded lever and starting by recoil and hand.

The ATC became an immediate best-seller, for it was irresistible, and once aboard the rider was quickly captivated. Fitted out with rear carrier and tow bar they could do sterling work on farm

The CB50 built in the style used by many other singles as marketed in a UK brochure

or woodland, so they also made their mark very firmly in the working world, where they could carry a man and his toolbox quickly and easily from place to place.

In 1971 the vertical engine theme was extended to a smaller size to produce the CB50. This used engine dimensions of 42 × 35·6 mm and produced 6 bhp at 10,500 rpm. Gaitered forks were fitted to the mainly tubular frame and in all it made a neat sporting package.

Also in the 50 cc class were the QA50 and PF50. The latter was an economy version of the PC50 and retained the ohv engine in a simple tube frame that lacked rear suspension and was fitted with light telescopic front forks. It was built in the Honda factory in Belgium and was known as the Graduate. In 1974 it gained pivoted fork rear suspension and was the forerunner of a number of basic mopeds built for the shopper and commuter.

The QA50 was totally different and built as a children's play bike, using the same 50 cc ohv engine with a two-speed gearbox. It had telescopic forks and a rigid tubular frame very similar to the Monkey bike. Like that model it had doughnut tyres and minimal mudguards.

The other two models new for 1971 were a self-start version of the middle step-thru, which became the C70M on the lines of the others, and the CT70, which was just an ST70 with a new type number.

1972 brought another model form, which again used the three-speed gearbox, automatic clutch, and camshaft engines to make the CF50 and CF70 Chaly machines. These used the small wheels from the ST or DAX series with an open step-thru beam frame fitted with telescopic forks. Small legshields were provided, so the result looked something of a ladies' model ST. The engine outputs were restricted in both cases.

In the 90 cc class the sports model was joined by a version fitted with a single disc front brake and typed CB90JX. To distinguish it further it received a new tank decor and side panel

graphics, which were then repeated on a drum-braked version, so Honda had three variants of a single model.

For 1972 Honda produced his largest single-cylinder machine since the ME of 1957 and also returned to the two-stroke cycle not seen since the F model Cub of 1952. Two new models were involved, both of 250 cc capacity, and both were to start new model lines for the firm.

The four-stroke was the SL250S and as the series letters indicated was built as a trail bike. In a few months it had changed its typing to the much better known XL250 and after it came a great range of similar models. From the start they featured a four-valve cylinder head with the single, chain-driven camshaft opening each pair of valves with a rocker with twin fingers. The

Left **A 1973 moped, the Novio or PM50, with very forward suspension unit**

Left below **The Novio in 1977 when its typing had grown to PF50DXR and its engine had become a four-stroke**

Bottom **And with automatic transmission and toothed belt drive there was the Camino built in Belgium**

Below **Meanwhile, the two-stroke became the PF50MR2 Amigo in 1977**

cambox was split on the camshaft centreline and the engine was all light alloy and built along the same lines of most Honda singles.

Thus the lubrication was wet sump, a centrifugal oil filter was attached to the end of the crankshaft, the generator and cam chain went on the left and the primary drive on the right. A five-speed gearbox was fitted and the cycle parts included a full cradle frame, telescopic front forks and pivoted fork rear suspension.

The machine came fully equipped for road or trail use so was no lightweight. For the casual rider this was fine as it made him feel more secure, and the machine sold well in the USA. It was less successful in Europe, where riders demanded more of it, and for the serious off-road man the solution was often to fit the engine unit, maybe tuned, into another chassis. For simply going anywhere it was hard to beat, as Terry Mentzer proved when he bought a 1976 model and rode round the world on it.

The two-stroke was a full-blooded motocross model typed the CR250 and called the Elsinore. Its engine was quite conventional with piston-controlled induction and four transfer ports. Dimensions were $70 \times 64 \cdot 4$ mm and actual compression ratio $7 \cdot 2{:}1$ with the power output 33 bhp at 7500 rpm. A flywheel magneto supplied the spark and lubrication was by petroil. The gearbox contained five speeds and the whole engine was very light and compact.

The frame was a single full loop with pivoted fork rear suspension and telescopic front forks. 140 mm drum brakes went into the wheels, the front shod with a $3 \cdot 00 \times 21$ in. tyre and the rear with a $4 \cdot 00 \times 18$ in. The detail fitments were as expected for a motocross machine and the weight a low 214 lb. It made an impact.

It was joined in 1973 by a smaller brother, the CR125, which was much the same but with electronic ignition and a six-speed gearbox. From these two motocross models Honda evolved a pair of enduro machines, the MT125 and MT250. Both were single-cylinder two-strokes, but detuned a little for serious off-road riding and competition. Both had five-speed gearboxes, high exhausts on the right and were equipped with lights, turn signals and horn to make them street legal.

For the off-road rider who wanted to compete in trials they introduced the TL125 and for this they retained the camshaft engine with suitable modifications to the power output and the gearing. For the motocross youngsters there was the XR75 with the 72 cc camshaft engine with the cylinder set near the vertical, a four-speed gearbox and tyre sizes reduced to 2·50 × 16 in. front and 3·00 × 14 in. rear. It came complete with black open exhaust and competition plates, so looked just the job.

The fun bike range was extended by fitting the 90 cc camshaft engine into the DAX frame to produce the ST90 and the upright 50 cc one in a tubular frame on similar lines to give the CY50. This differed in that it had a downtube to the frame and conventional fuel tank, but it retained the fat tyres.

On the road models the CB50 was offered with a disc front brake and for the special needs of the UK market the SS50 was built with a four-speed gearbox and pedals. Thanks to these it then qualified as a moped, so could be ridden at 16 years old. The pedals were contrived so that they could both be locked forward to act as footrests or could, with some difficulty, be used to propel the machine. This class of machine, known as 'sixteener specials', was simply a way around the regulations and they were dropped in 1977 when the rules were amended, but not before the five-speed, disc-brake model had reached the UK in 1975.

Last of the new models for 1973 was another moped with a two-stroke engine and automatic transmission by belt and variable pulleys. This was the PM50 with simple beam frame, leading link forks and short, forward-mounted, rear suspension units.

1974 brought another miniature motocross

Basic but good, the Honda Express moped

model in the form of the MR50. This followed the lines of the XR75 but with a two-stroke engine, three-speed gearbox and spine frame. It was built for children and to suit their ability the throttle stop could be set to one of four positions by the parents.

For users of the 72 cc camshaft engine there were two new models. For trail use came the XL70, in essence a new name for the earlier SL70, itself derived from the CL70 but using the tubular frame of the SL series with the horizontal engine. The XL continued the theme with detail changes only. The second model was the ATC70, another three-wheeled fun bike with balloon tyres just like the 90 cc version. It sold just as well.

The remaining 1974 models were all in the XL series and thus for trail use. The 250 was now well established and was joined by three more in 125, 175 and 350 cc sizes. All followed the same lines with single overhead camshaft, but only the largest had four valves. Before long there was a whole array of extras available for the XL series in America to pull the weight down, give it a power boost or make the machine more suited to enduro work.

The TL125 also began to come under scrutiny that year when Sammy Miller signed a contract to develop the trials models. The basic engine remained, but the detail work and the chassis all received attention. In 1975 it was joined by the TL250, which went through the same programme to move on from its XL250 parentage.

An equally basic commuter model, the CG125 with ohv but otherwise much as the camshaft models

In 1975 the 125 single was modified in detail and renamed the CB125J and two more mopeds appeared. One was the Novio and was a development of the PF50 with rear suspension and a fuel tank on the main frame. The other was the PF50MR, or Amigo, and in the same concept as the PM50. Like that model it had a two-stroke engine and an automatic clutch, but the frame was a single tube and fitted with simple telescopics and rear suspension.

In 1976 more mopeds appeared called Camino and Road Express, to be followed in time

The C50 in 1984, little changed since the first Super Cub of 1958

by more in both moped and scooter form. Models such as the Melody and Caren were brought in along with the stylish MB50 and MT50 for road and trail. Such machines and many more reflected the trends and styles of the eighties and Honda was as always at the front of the market.

Before the decade ended the trials model range was taken down in size to the TL50 and this was joined by two enduro machines, the XE50 and XE75. All used the camshaft single engine and cycle parts to suit their purpose, with the two XE models on small wheels to suit young riders and with four-speed gearboxes. The trail machine range was extended with the five-speed XL100, and new enduro machines appeared.

These were the MR175 and MR250 built for serious enduro use, so closer to the CR

motocross machines than the MT, which were for serious trail riding rather than enduros. Thus the rider was offered XL, XR, MT, MR and CR models for off-road use from dual-purpose to full competition. Some confusion arose, not only because of the number of machines but also because CR models in the early days had been road-racing machines built on a production basis. The difficulty in now having a CR motocross model was compounded by the appearance of the MT125R, which was a two-stroke road racer and not another version of the trail bike.

The MR models were based firmly on the CR ones, the 175 model being produced by boring the engine out. Both had five-speed gearboxes, which were enough for enduro work, and detail parts came from XL, CR and MT models to suit.

In 1976 Honda added the CT125 to the list of camshaft singles and this one was based on the XL but adapted for farm use. To this end the protection for both rider and machine was extended and a massive rear carrier provided to help with the carriage of equipment. Such machines were popular on the vast farms of Australia, but in time were superseded by the ATC.

For the commuter the CG125 was introduced as a rock-bottom machine with ohv engine and four- or five-speed gearbox. It was a simple and sensible machine, also built as the 105 cc model CG110, with full chaincase, drum brakes, mirrors and minimal servicing needs.

It ran on into the eighties with many more of the singles—the XLs which took to twin exhaust pipes and a 500 cc thumper, a derived XR series, a 250 cc road single using the camshaft engine, a 100 cc two-stroke and many more.

But the mainstay of the business, the step-thru, just continued with its job of providing transport.

3 | Twins in all sizes

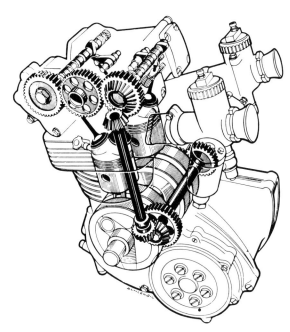

Inspiration—the NSU works Rennmax much admired by Soichiro Honda in 1954

From Edwardian times it was known that one route to increased power was to use more cylinders and run the engine faster. In 1957, Soichiro Honda decided to go that way and launched his first twin-cylinder motorcycle and was to set a pattern for many more.

The model was the C70 and very modern it was too with its all-aluminium engine unit built in one with the gearbox and with the cylinders inclined forward a little. Bore and stroke were equal at 54 mm so the capacity was 247 cc, and on an 8·2:1 compression ratio it produced 18 bhp at 7400 rpm.

The two pistons rose and fell together in the classic twin-cylinder pattern and a single, chain-driven overhead camshaft was used. The drive to it was taken from the centre of the crankshaft and passed up through tunnels in the cylinder block and head under the control of various guide rollers and tensioners.

The crankshaft was pressed together and ran on four ball-bearing mains. The big ends were rollers and the small ends carried three-ring pistons. The camshaft ran in the head and rockers communicated its form to the valves, while an ignition cam and an advance mechanism went on to the left camshaft end. Outboard of them went a distributor to direct the high-tension current to the correct spark plug.

The alternator went on the right end of the crankshaft and the clutch on the left so it ran at engine speed. The lift mechanism went outboard of the main cases under a separate small cover, from the rear of which the operating cable emerged. Gear primary drive was used and the mainshaft of the gearbox was extended to the left to carry a centrifugal oil filter, simply a hollow drum through which the oil passed.

The gearbox contained four speeds and was of the cross-over design with the output sprocket mounted on a sleeve gear on the right that was concentric with the mainshaft. Thus the gearbox was not all-indirect and its layshaft lay behind the mainshaft. Gears were selected by forks controlled by a barrel cam and the positive stop mechanism went on the left, as did the foot

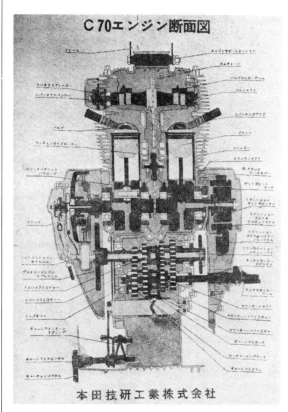

First Honda twin engine, the 1957 C70 with overhead camshaft and engine speed clutch

pedal. The kickstarter was on the right and the drive chain was fully enclosed by a chaincase.

The engine unit was mounted in a spine frame built up from deep section pressings and was supported at the rear of the crankcase and from a lug cast into the top of the cambox. The frame continued to the rear to form the rear mudguard and down to support the pivoted rear fork, the rear of the engine and the centre stand. Openings were formed in each side to accommodate the electrics and the oil tank for the dry sump system also went into the frame with the filler cap on the right.

The front forks were similar to those used for the camshaft singles with short leading links and the spring units hidden within the legs. The forks were again built up from pressings welded together and they had a rather unusual rectangular section styling profile. This was repeated by the rear suspension units, the headlamp shell and, to a lesser degree, the fuel tank. The rear pivoted fork was again built up from pressings.

Both wheels had full-width, light-alloy hubs with single leading shoe brakes and the front back plate floated and was restrained by a torque stay.

The wheels were built up with wire spokes and steel rims and both carried 3·25 × 16 in. tyres. The mudguards were generous in their size and protection.

A cantilever saddle was provided for the rider and behind that a carrier with grab handle was bolted to the rear mudguard. A pillion pad could be fixed to this carrier and passenger footrests were attached to the rear fork arms.

The handlebars were shrouded by a pressing to conceal the cables and wiring and this principle was continued in the area behind the cylinders with a cast alloy cover on each side. Equipment was very comprehensive with a speedometer set in the top of the headlamp housing, the ignition switch in its left side, a mirror and small turn indicators. The standard of design of the electrics and their controls set the

The C71 at Amsterdam in 1959, the first time it had been seen in Europe

style that was to come from the East from then on.

The twin was modified for 1958 and became the C71, with an electric starter mounted in front of the crankcase. It drove the crankshaft with a short chain that connected to a sprocket and roller clutch fitted inboard of the alternator. It was joined by two further models using the same basic engine unit, but with a raised compression ratio of 9:1 and an increase in power to 20 bhp at 8400 rpm.

The first was the CS71, which was otherwise as the tourer except that to go with the extra power there was a dualseat and a raised exhaust system on each side. These were masked by perforated heat shields and with them out of the way the curved kickstart lever of the C70 could be replaced with a straight one.

The second new model was the RC70f and a complete scrambler, not a road version at all, although it was possible to fit the high-level

exhaust systems and lights to make it street legal. The engine was without the electric starter of the C71 and its twin exhaust pipes both curled around to the right and ran along high up to open ends. A small heat shield was fitted to protect the rider's right calf.

The frame was completely new and all tubular with a cradle running under the engine to protect it as much as to support it. The front forks were of the long leading link, or Earles, type and were built from tubing with the link fork being formed from a single tube as a hairpin. At the rear was a pivoted fork and this was controlled by units that were further forward and laid down to a degree to improve wheel movement and control.

Braced handlebars were fitted, the seat was fairly short and the mudguards were brief. Tyres were studded, but the front was only of 19 in. diameter, not the 21 in. that was more usual for such models.

The 250 cc models were joined by more twins in three capacities, two smaller and one larger. The smallest was the C90, which was in essence a reduced scale C70. The capacity was 124·7 cc from 44 × 41 mm dimensions and on an 8·5:1

compression ratio it produced 11·5 bhp at 9500 rpm. The cycle parts duplicated the 250, but were all slightly smaller to suit the capacity. Differences were that the primary drive went on the right and the final on the left in the classic Honda twin layout.

With the tourer came the CB90, which was a far more sporting model. A hump-backed tank with knee pads and recesses replaced the angular standard item, a trim dualseat was fitted and low flat bars went with a small screen attached to the top of the headlamp shell. A twin leading shoe front brake was fitted with the cable working the two cam levers, while the leading link forks were retained. The rear suspension units were left exposed and the exhaust pipes

The sports twin built as the CS71 and CS76 in 1958–59

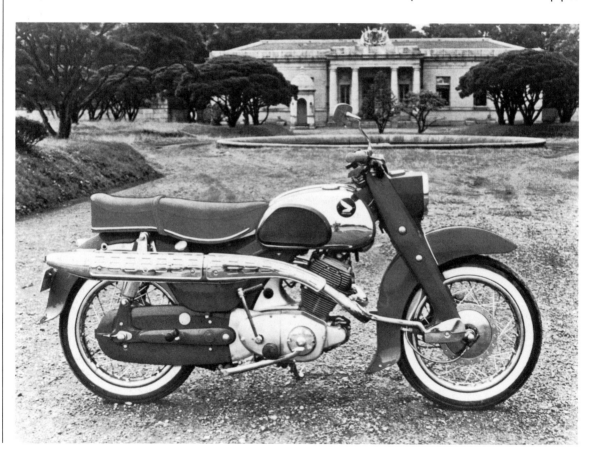

The CS72 with wet-sump lubrication in 1961, still a curious mix with massive mudguards and upswept exhaust systems

terminated in long, shallow taper megaphone silencers.

Slightly larger were the touring C95 and sports CB95, which repeated the features of the two 125 cc models. The difference lay in the engine, which was bored out to 49 mm and 154 cc. Compression ratios for the two models were 8·6 and 10:1 and power outputs 13·5 bhp at 9500 rpm and 16·5 bhp at 10,000 rpm. The sports machine had 18 in. wheels while the tourer kept to the 16 in.

The two larger machines were based on the 250s and their 305 cc capacity was reached by boring the engine to 60 mm. The models were the touring C75 and the CS76 with raised exhaust systems and electric start. They thus mirrored the C70 and CS71 and the tourer became the C76 in 1960 with the addition of the starter motor as on the C71.

In 1959 the 125s became the C92 and CB92 to be joined by a third model, the CS92. Respectively, they were the tourer, the super-sports and the tourer with raised exhausts as in earlier years and remained much as the earlier models. They continued the angular styling and it was the first two of this trio that were to be seen in Europe within a couple of years. With their very full specification and equipment, excellent finish and attention to detail they quickly made an impact which was augmented by keen pricing.

The handling and road holding of the machines from the East lacked the precision and control of the European ones and it was to be a long

Right **The 125 cc CB92 super sports model in 1961**

Below **The 1961 C92 touring twin with Maicoletta scooter in the background. At that time Maico importers also handled Honda in the UK**

time before those aspects were fully dealt with. But in the showroom Honda brought a new image to motorcycling and the good electrics, silence and lack of oil leaks all went a long way to selling the machines to the general public.

Even if the traditional rider frowned on the handling he had to admire the engines. They ran at speeds only used for road racing, seemed to be unburstable and kept their oil inside. It took a long time for even the press, let alone the public, to become used to running at the high speeds needed to keep the little twins on the boil. Those that learned this found a whole new world of riding opening up before them.

Two 250s appeared in 1959, one, the CB71, was a super sports model on the lines of the CB90. The second was the CR71, which was built as a road racer with lights. It retained many of the C70 features, but the front brake became a

two leading shoe device with the cam levers joined by a link, the seat was dual or a racing one with a hump, the front mudguard very narrow and close fitting, extending a long way round the tyre like an early works MV, but even when racing the kickstart lever was retained. The forks remained leading links and the engine speed clutch was retained, but the power was up to 24 bhp at 8800 rpm.

1960 brought a revised design for the 250 with the appearance of the C72 and its derivatives, the CB72 and CS72. The cycle parts remained as on the C70 and the general theme was the same, but the engine changed to wet-sump

1961 CB72 on show in Japan, Twin carburettors, 180-degree crankshaft, tubular frame and telescopic forks all differed from the tourer

<sidebar>Honda—The Early Classic Motorcycles</sidebar>

Above **The 1962 M85 Juno scooter with flat twin-engine and variable-ratio hydraulic transmission**

Left **Juno engine with twin carburettors and hydraulic valve tappets**

lubrication as nearly all Hondas were to use from then on.

The engine dimensions remained as for the C70, but the power was up to 20 bhp at 8000 rpm for the C72 and 24 bhp at 9000 rpm for the CB72. The CS72 continued the theme of using the touring engine with high-rise pipes, and, in this case, whitewall tyres.

The engine design was a development of the earlier model complete with its electric starter

Above **Sporting CL72 trail model in 1963 with stylish exhausts. Juno scooter stands behind**

Right **1964 CB92 engine unit in its spine frame. Note blanked-off rev-counter drive commented on at the time during road test**

and single carburettor. The transmission was altered with the clutch moving to the gearbox mainshaft and being driven by chain on the left. The gearbox layout remained the same, so the final drive chain continued to be on the right.

The base of the horizontally split crankcase was extended to accommodate the oil and well finned to keep it cool. The gear pump was assembled to a casting that bolted to the underside of the crankcase and this held its drive pinion

Specifications for the Honda 305 Super Sport			
Engine—Cylinders: Twin 4-stroke	Transmission—Clutch: Wet multiplate	Brakes—Front: T.L.S.	
Bore & stroke: 60 mm x 54 mm	Overall Gear Ratios—1st: 17.46:1	Rear: T.L.S.	
Capacity: 305 c.c.	2nd: 10.42:1	Tyres—Front: 2.75 x 18	
Com. Ratio: 9.5:1	3rd: 7.53:1	Rear: 3.00 x 18	
Valve operation: O.H.C.	Top: 6.27:1	Performance—B.H.P.: 28.5 at 9,000 RPM	
Ignition: Battery & coil	Suspension—Front: Telescopic	Max. torque: 2.5 kgm at 7,000 RPM	
Lubrication: Wet Sump	Rear: Pivot fork	Max. speed: 90 m.p.h.	
Starting method: Kick & electric	Weight: 350 lbs	Price (inc. P.T.): £269.19.0	

Who will win the CC vs RPM war?

There are men who still believe that the more cc's they've got the better the bike. It's the old myth that engine capacity is synonymous with power. Honda owners disagree—violently. A high-revving Honda will give a big 500 c.c a run for its money any day—and still have lots of change left over.

Honda's fantastically high rpm is a result of superior engineering. Instruments with a .0001" diamond stylus probe microscopic hills on metal surfaces that appear as smooth as glass to a micrometer. They set the exacting standards for all Honda components. Engineering such as this accounts for the miracle of high rpm. And results in Honda winning all those races.

For instance, with a Honda 305 Super Sport you can cruise forever at 75 mph at about 6,500 rpm... and have a lot of rpm's left for hitting the top.

But don't take our word for it—the man who tested a Honda 305 Super Sport for MOTOR CYCLING put it this way: "The conception of the sporting roadster as a contraption necessarily rather stark, rather noisy and rather intractable is dead, buried and patted down flat." So that's that.

Just the same, Honda doesn't have anything against those big cc machines ...there's a place for them.

The Honda 305 Super Sport costs only £269.19.0 (That's something else you can compare with those big bikes.)

the one that's reliable
Power Road, Chiswick, London, W.4.

Left **One of a series of Honda UK advertisements that annoyed many British machine traditionalists due to their use of thinly disguised Vincent (here) and BSA twins**

Right **1965 C95, a 150 cc twin similar to its larger and smaller brothers**

in mesh with one cut on the crankshaft centre.

The centrifugal oil filter was retained, but space precluded it being fitted to the crankshaft. So it was mounted ahead of this in the primary chaincase and driven from a sprocket right on the end of the crankshaft by a short chain. In all there were thus five chains in the twin, for oil filter, starter, camshaft, primary and final drives.

The chassis side of the C72 and CS72 continued in the rather ponderous style of the C70 with pressed-steel frame, forks, rear fork and chaincase. The angular styling remained and with it the luxury touring image. For all that, and a weight just over 350 lb dry, on test it was able to just better 80 mph and in 1960 that was a very creditable figure. The suspension was very touring and soft so the handling was poor on fast, bumpy bends, but of an acceptable nature to many of its customers. It was a complaint that was to take two decades to completely solve, although progress was made even in the early days. A change of rear suspension units often worked wonders and became *sine qua non* among the hard riders in Europe and the USA.

The CB72 was a different machine in many ways. The engine looked like a twin-carburettor version of the tourer, but inside it went a 180-degree crankshaft. This and the resultant uneven breathing did in truth dictate the two intakes and twin contact breakers controlled by a single cam on the right end of the camshaft. This was of two-piece construction, as on the C72, with each half carrying two cams and splining to the

central drive sprocket. The compression ratio was up to 9·5:1, but in other respects the engine and transmission duplicated the tourer. The frame did not. It was all tubular but constructed in spine form to mirror the form of the pressed-steel one. Three tubes ran back from the head-stock to a braced junction through which the top tube ran before curving down to the rear fork pivot area. Tubes ran back and up to the rear units and bracing plates welded them all together and replaced the forged lug and its brazing of the past.

A further change came at the front end with the adoption of telescopic forks with neat shrouds with small ears to support the headlamp shell. The rear chaincase was replaced by a small

Left **The touring C72 in 1965 complete with tyre pump beneath seat**

Below **Start of a very long line, the CB160 which grew in turn to 175 and then 200. This is a 1965 model**

chainguard and suitable lugs and brackets were added to the frame's midriff to support the electrics, which were hidden by side covers.

The hubs continued to be full width and in light alloy, but both brakes became twin leading shoe devices with an external link joining the cam levers. The wheel size became 18 in. and the tyre sections 2·75 in. front and 3·00 in. rear. Mudguards were narrow and sporting, especially at the front, while the rear one was more deeply valanced.

The angular styling went, but the humpy tank stayed with a very comfortable dualseat. The footrests were attached to stylish, forged, light-alloy plates on each side of the machine and held

to radially serrated bosses by single fixing bolts. They could thus be easily adjusted for position and the same idea, and plate, also supported the pillion rests.

A third boss in each plate gave an alternative footrest position and the rear brake pedal and gear lever were both designed to locate with their respective footrest and thus move position with it. To further assist fast riding the bars were short and flat with a combined speedometer and rev counter, driven from the camshaft, set in front of them in the top of the headlamp shell.

No turn signals were fitted to the first models, although they appeared later, but otherwise the equipment was comprehensive. It proved to be

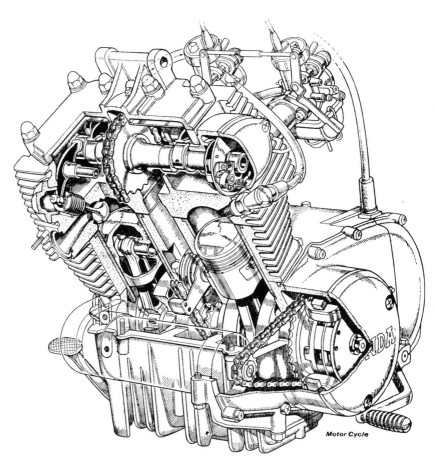

**CB160 engine with single
camshaft, 360-degree
crankshaft and electric starter
with chain drive on left**

Motor Cycle

a fast machine with a top speed just on 90 mph, good brakes and improved handling. They were popular and while often a little more expensive than other 250s they were cheaper than anything else that offered the same performance.

In 1961, a derivative, the CBM72, appeared with high bars and turn signals and it was joined in 1962 by the CL72. This was a trail model rather on the lines of the RC70 but fitted out to be street legal. It used the CB72 engine unit in a tubular cradle frame with both exhausts routed high on the left. Telescopic front forks were fitted with a straight line hydraulic steering damper, and the equipment included high bars, narrow mudguards with the front still close-fitting and

Right **A pair of Black Bombers as the CB450 was known when it was launched**

Below **Road racer Dave Degens on the CB450 during a track test session**

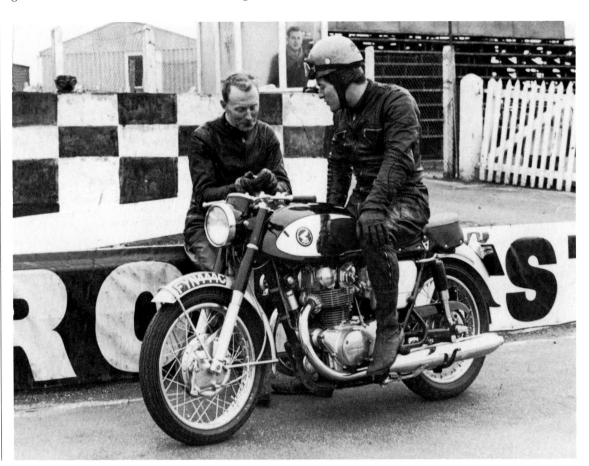

19 in. wheels carrying trail tyres. Brakes were single leading shoe and only a speedometer was supplied. Under the frame and crankcase went a bash-plate and the footrests were cleated, hinged but spring-loaded, and held to a separate mounting bar.

For a trail machine the CL72 was big, heavy and clumsy, really much more a street scrambler for use on the tarmac than off it, but it introduced many Americans to the delights of trail riding as a casual relaxation rather than a do-or-die challenge. It was fun, so the machine sold. Along with it the road model became the Hawk in the USA and won many converts.

1962 also saw the final form for a very different Honda twin. This had the two cylinders set horizontally opposed and the engine was used for a scooter. It had first appeared two years earlier

as the M80 and this was of 125 cc capacity with equal bore and stroke at 43 mm. On a 9:1 compression ratio it developed 11 bhp at 9000 rpm. By 1962 it had become the M85 of 169 cc by an increase in bore size to 50 mm. This pushed the power up to 12 bhp at a lower engine speed of 7600 rpm.

It was a complex machine with many novel features, which was why it was never sold outside Japan. The lines of communication for spares and servicing would have been too stretched. One or two models did escape and attracted a good deal of attention when seen.

The engine had a built-up crankshaft with caged roller big ends and plain small ones. The crankcase and transmission split on the vertical centreline and each head and barrel was separate. Overhead valves were used with the cam-

Right **A C77 calling on a Colchester dealer for a service during a ride from Beirut to Dublin**

Left **CB450 advertisement showing some details and the combined instruments**

Right **Line drawing of the twin overhead camshaft engine with its torsion bar valve springs**

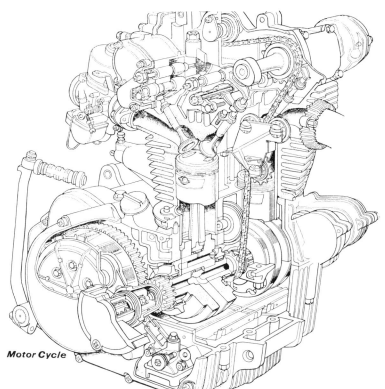

Motor Cycle

77

shaft on the engine centreline, chain driven, and the valve gear comprised pushrods and hydraulic tappets in the cylinder heads to absorb the clearances and reduce engine noise. Ignition was by coil, with a skew-driven points housing angled up on the left of the crankcase, and an electric starter was provided. As a back-up, a hand-pull, recoil manual starter was fitted.

The transmission was a variable ratio hydraulic system based on Badalini patents. This used a swashplate and hydraulic motor in place of a gearbox, and a second twistgrip, on the left, adjusted the ratio by altering the swashplate angle. A common technique in the hydraulics industry but not in motorcycles. The rest of the transmission was by chain, sprockets and bevels to reach the rear wheel and give the necessary overall reduction ratio.

The chassis construction was fairly typical scooter modified to fit the engine up near the front wheel just ahead of the apron. This improved the weight distribution and with 3·50 × 10 in. tyres and trailing link front suspension the handling was better than that of the Italian machines of the day, then the norm.

The scooter, known as the Juno, had unusual lines with the apron flared back to clear the engine and a good-sized central tunnel to accommodate the transmission. The front mudguard was massive, the rear panels narrow

with the rear units on the outside and a seat and carrier, or a dualseat, on top. The headlamp moved with the bars and winkers were fitted, but there was no windscreen, which was unusual for a scooter.

For 1963 four new 305 cc models appeared labelled C77, C78, CB77 and CP77. In the USA the sports model was named the Super Hawk. All used the C76 engine and the first two were tourers nearly identical to the older machine and the C72. Thus they retained the angular style, leading link front forks and 16 in. wheels. The C78 had raised tubular bars which replaced the pressed steel plus tube ends of the C77. Both used the single-carburettor engine, which produced 23 bhp at 7500 rpm on an 8·2:1 compression ratio.

The CB77 was a near copy of the Hawk 250 so had the 180-degree crank, telescopic fork, tubular spine frame and uprated engine. Compression ratio became 9·5:1 and power went to 28·5 bhp at 9000 rpm. That was enough to push it along at 95 mph and the machine retained most, if not all, of the features of the CB72. This included a kickstarter pedal that moved forwards when it was needed, but in practice this was never as the electric starter worked well.

The CP77 was just another version of the CB model with high bars, just like the CBM72. All these models in 125, 150, 250 and 305 cc forms ran on to around 1967 with detail improvements

Left **Controls and instruments of a 1967 CB72 with vertical distance recorder**

Right above **A Honda twin running in the 1967 500-mile race at Brands Hatch with open-ended, high-level exhaust system**

Right **The CB125 twin in 1967, a very typical Honda model of that period**

year by year but without any major change. The one feature that did receive attention was the 180-degree crankshaft of the two larger models, which was changed to 360 degree with appropriate alterations to the ignition system. For a while both versions were offered.

In 1964 the sports 125 cc twin became the CB93 and followed its larger brethren to telescopic front forks and a tubular spine frame. The engine remained as before, but the appearance was very different from the angular lines of the earlier model. With it that year came the CB160 and this was set in the same style with an enlarged engine. The capacity was 161 cc achieved by boring the engine out to 50 mm. Power was 16·5 bhp at 10,000 rpm on an 8·5:1 compression ratio and the cycle parts were as for the smaller sports twin.

The engine reflected the archetypal Honda twin with its 360-degree pressed-up crankshaft and single overhead camshaft driven by a central chain. The crankcase was split horizontally on the centreline of the crank and gearbox shafts with covers on each side. The cylinders were cast in light alloy in one block with pressed-in liners and the head was also a one-piece casting incorporating the cam box. It was sealed by a lid at the top and eight long studs ran up to this from the crankcase with dome nuts at the top.

The stud holes also acted as oil pipes to convey the lubricant up to the camshaft and rockers.

The camshaft was forged in one with the sprocket at the centre and ran directly in light alloy end covers. These were located on to the ends of the two rocker shafts on each side and also held these in place. The rockers carried adjusters at their outer end with access via typical Honda valve caps. On the left end of the camshaft went a twin-lobe ignition cam driven via an advance mechanism and this controlled a single pair of points. These fired a battery-powered double coil so that every time the pistons came up both plugs fired. As a system it gave no trouble and it made timing easy. The alternator rotor was marked with T and F for top dead centre and ignition fire. The camshaft sprocket was also marked and if aligned at tdc was set correctly.

The alternator went on the left with a starter clutch inboard of it and driven from a motor bolted to the front of the crankcase. On the right went the primary drive by gear and both members of the pair were duplicated, with the teeth staggered and the gears spring-loaded for quiet running. The clutch was a conventional multiplate and lifted by a pushrod moved by a quick thread on the left. The adjuster for this screwed into a block which slid into a recess in

Far left **The first CD175 in 1967 with well-inclined engine and pressed-steel frame. A model build in large numbers**

Left **Engine unit of the 1967 SS125 twin which had the cam chain on the left of the barrel and not central**

Below **The CS125 on show at Tokyo in 1967 with a P25 behind**

the crankcase side and thanks to this the cable was easy to disconnect.

The clutch body was also the oil pump drive, with an eccentric machined on to its rear face. This worked a plunger pump bolted to the crankcase side beneath the crankshaft and the oil was fed into the shaft via a centrifugal oil filter. Access to this for cleaning was via a small cover set in the main primary drive cover. The system was wet sump with the oil carried in the finned lower crankcase and used to lubricate engine and transmission.

The gearbox was of the cross-over, all-indirect type, so the final drive chain went on the left.

Left **A CB350 twin on show in Holland in 1968**

Right **Trail 350 twin in 1969, the SL350 with black exhausts and a steering damper**

Below **Several Hondas in a line in 1968 with a CB450 in the forefront**

As befitted a sports machine it was exposed under a small guard. The gears were selected by a barrel cam and the positive stop mechanism went behind the clutch on the right, but its shaft extended across the engine and out on the left.

Twin carburettors and exhaust systems were fitted, the latter retained by a collar and split clamp arrangement that allowed the collar to be removed from the exhaust pipe despite the attached silencer. The whole engine was very easy to work on and could be quickly dropped out of the frame for bench operation. Special tools were kept to a minimum. The rear wheel spindle could double as an alternator rotor puller, the clutch drum was only held by a circlip and the gearbox sprocket by two small bolts. Only the crankshaft gear nut was special as it lived at the bottom of the oil filter and required a four-key Honda tool. This was not expensive, but if not available a workshop could adapt welding wire and a socket spanner to cope with the job. The rest was nuts and bolts.

The CB160 engine used the tubular spine frame and telescopic front forks common to the sports Hondas. The front brake had twin leading shoes, the rear a single, and both wheels had 18 in. rims. It was a smart machine with the refinements of mirror, dualseat, good electrics and no oil leaks, now expected as normal for the make. It proved to be good for just under 80 mph and able to cruise at 70 mph for most of the time. Brakes were very good and the handling much improved on that of the early models with leading links.

The next Honda twin to come on to the scene represented several new steps forward for the firm. The machine was the CB450 Dream and it was launched in April 1965. At that time it became the largest-capacity production Honda and both engine and frame included new features along with many common to the twins.

The special points of the engine were the 180-degree crankshaft, twin overhead camshafts driven by one long bush chain and torsion-bar

Above **1973 CD175 for riding to work, for which it was very well suited**

Above left **The more sporting CB175 in 1972**

Below **The trail big twin, a 1972 CL450 with entwined exhaust pipes at high level but close-fitting front mudguard**

valve springs. The engine was well over-square with dimensions of 70 × 57·8 mm, which made the capacity 444·9 cc but allowed it to run to 8500 rpm, at which speed it produced 43 bhp on an 8·5:1 compression ratio.

Engine construction followed the lines of the smaller twins, so the crankshaft was built up with caged roller big ends and the crankcase split horizontally. The cylinders were cast in one block, the heads in another, both in light alloy, and the cam chain ran up the centre of both. The cam boxes were both cast in one with the head and each camshaft ran in light alloy end caps bolted to the sides.

The valve springs were the most unusual feature of the engine. The valves were made in the usual way and machined to take a collar located by split collets as normal. An arm with a forked end was positioned under the collar and was splined to a tube. The end of the tube was internally splined and into this went the end of the torsion bar, simply a length of steel of closely controlled diameter expanded into a spline at each end. At its outer end it entered a second tube, which was made with a locating arm. By winding this round it loaded the torsion bar and, via the tube and forked arm, the valve. A single bolt held it in this loaded position and as the valve opened so the torsion bar was wound up further. Really no different to a coil valve spring which also works in torsion. Only the installation was different.

The appearance of the system, uncannily like a desmodromic one in looks, was augmented by the use of finger followers between each cam and its valve. These were mounted on eccentric shafts whose rotation enabled the valve clearance to be set.

The camshaft drive involved one endless chain and numerous sprockets and guide rollers. Immediately above the crankshaft was a roller with the chain running against each side. Next, in the cylinder block, was a fixed sprocket at the front and a tensioner at the rear. These sprockets

acted to guide the chain out towards the camshafts, and the tensioner was spring-loaded from an adjustable set position.

Above these, at the base of the cylinder head, went a free-running sprocket at the rear and a pair of free rollers at the front. From these the chain ran to and from the camshaft sprockets and between these went a central jockey which increased the sprocket wrap.

The ignition cam went on the left end of the exhaust camshaft with a single lobe opening twin sets of points at the uneven firing intervals dictated by the 180-degree crank. For the rest the engine was stock Honda with alternator and final drive on the left, primary drive on the right, four-speed all-indirect gearbox, plunger oil pump driven by an eccentric on the back of the clutch drum and wet sump.

Two carburettors of the constant-velocity type were fitted with vacuum pistons and butterfly throttles. Another new departure for Honda.

The cycle side was also different, for in place of the spine frame there was a cradle, and thanks to this the cylinders were set vertical and lost their inclination. Suspension was conventional, as were most of the other chassis details, with a twin leading shoe front brake, full equipment and a combined speedometer and rev counter, the latter driven from the exhaust camshaft.

The result was called the black bomber to reflect its black finish, which was relieved only by the silver of the mudguards and side covers, and chrome tank panels. It was also banned from English production racing as it had twin overhead camshafts; it was suggested that only road racing engines had such esoteric features despite the bland way it ripped up to just over 100 mph and covered the standing quarter in the 14-second bracket.

April 1965 was the beginning of the end for the British motorcycle industry. Up until then they had comforted themselves with the thought that the Japanese only sold small motorcycles. With the advent of a big model in the 500 cc class from the world's largest manufacturer their protective bubble burst. Hard on the heels of the CB450 were to come other big machines, fast and exciting, from Kawasaki, Suzuki and Yamaha, with more from Honda. No longer would the learner progress from his small Honda to a big Triumph, it was a lesson that Meriden and Small Heath had forgotten, but it was well learned in Tokyo and Hamamatsu.

In 1966, the existing 125 cc models were replaced by three new ones, the CB125, CL125 and CD125. These were respectively sports, street scrambler and tourer as indicated by their prefix letters and all used the well-inclined engine as before. The compression ratio of the CB was

Above right **The CB250 in 1973 with disc front brake**

Right **The larger CB350 from the same year but different styling and drum brakes**

Below **A CL350, more a street scrambler than a trail bike, from a 1973 advertisement**

higher than the others and all three developed differing power outputs.

The CB continued the tubular spine frame and other features of the CB93 and the CL model was very similar but with the narrower mudguards, heavier tyre sections and raised exhausts on the left usual to the type. The CD125 had a much more touring image and used the pressed-steel frame of the past updated to the T-spine form used by a number of the singles. The wheels were smaller at 16 in. diameter and the touring lines were accentuated by well-valanced mudguards, a full chaincase, fat silencers and a separate seat plus a pillion pad fitted to the rear carrier. Telescopic forks were used, but only a single leading shoe drum brake at the front.

The 125s were joined by the CL77 that year

and this was in street scrambler guise and much as the smaller 250, although the exhausts at least did vary. For 1967 it was renamed the CL300, and after that year all the Honda twins changed to a numbering system comprising the letter prefix to indicate its basic use, the nominal engine capacity and suffixes to identify model changes.

There were other changes in 1967 for the 125 cc twins, and in all eight variations were on offer. The three from 1966 were joined by new versions and additions. Thus there was the CD125A, which was altered only by the use of a single seat in place of the dual. The second CB125 was also a seat amendment and in its case this became a racing item with rear hump. The CL125A adopted the T-spine frame with the rest as was and the SS125 was a new model using the same engine and frame with low exhausts and standard handlebars. Finally there was the CS125, much as the CD with spine frame and 16 in. wheels but with a little more power.

Confused? Well so were the dealers!

In 1967 they also saw the first examples of one of Honda's long runners, the CD175. This was to become a minor classic and the motorcycle for commuting if a C50 was too small. I had one as a town bike for five years and for that job it was superb, slim and nimble in traffic, fast enough to keep ahead of the stream and dead reliable.

The first of them was a combination of parts from the CB160 and CD125. The engine capacity came from boring it out to 52 mm while still keeping to the 41 mm stroke. Engine design followed the well-worn Honda path and went with a single carburettor and a four-speed gearbox. No electric starter was fitted, although the mountings were there along with the extension of the alternator cover to enclose the drive chain.

The frame was the T-spine fitted with telescopic forks, 16 in. wheels, full-width hubs, deep mudguards and a full chaincase. Equipment included turn indicators, mirrors and a good dualseat, but the six-volt headlamp was too small and weak for use outside a lighted area.

With the road model came the CL175, and this was fitted with the same engine in the tubular spine frame and with high-level exhausts on the left. For riders who wanted a more powerful street scrambler there came the CL450 based on the black bomber but with a raised exhaust system on each side, wide and braced bars plus spring-loaded footrests among its off-road fitments.

1968 brought the CB175, which was simply an enlarged 160 complete with its twin carburettors and tubular spine frame. At the same time a completely new range of medium-sized twins was introduced in a style that was to be used many more times. The new machines comprised three 250s and a pair of 350s. All were based on a common crankshaft with 50·6 mm stroke with the smaller engine having a 56 mm bore and 249·3 cc capacity, while the larger went to 64 mm and 325·6 cc.

The smaller twins were the sporting CB250 producing 30 bhp at 10,500 rpm and the street scrambler CL250 and touring CD250, both of which had to manage with 27 bhp and 10,000 rpm. The larger models were the CB350 with 36 bhp at 10,500 rpm and the CL350 with 33 bhp at 9500 rpm. All five engines shared a compression ratio set at 9·5:1.

The engine was developed from the earlier twins with many features from them, but its appearance was altered by setting the cylinders close to the vertical with just a touch of forward inclination. The cranks were set at 180 degrees and the four mains, central chain drive to the single overhead camshaft, alternator on left, gear primary drive on right, electric starter at the front and ignition cam on the end of the camshaft were all standard Honda practice.

The engine top end differed in that the cambox was separate from the cylinder head, the camshaft sprocket was bolted to the shaft and the rockers were on eccentrics that rotated to set the valve clearance. The bottom half followed form except that five speeds were provided for the CB and CL models, although the CD had to manage with four.

The cycle parts for all five models were very similar, with the frame a tubular cradle one with some pressings used for the area behind the engine. Telescopic front forks were used, fitted with gaiters for the CL models, but otherwise with shrouds. All models had the same size wheels and tyres and a twin leading shoe front brake went on to the sports machines. They also had separate instruments, unlike the CD, which had a speedometer only and a home market CB which shared this feature and the same general finish.

The big twin, the 450, was changed in 1968 with an additional gear in the box as the CB450K1 and the street scrambler received the same benefit. It also altered its exhaust so that both pipes ran up on the left to twin silencers in the pattern common for the CL series.

The three basic forms of the 125 cc twin, the CB, CL and CD, all changed their engine style in 1969. The cylinders came back to nearly vertical, just like the new range 250 and 350, and a similar tubular frame was adopted. The CB125

was given a five-speed gearbox, but in most respects the machines remained the same models but with very different looks.

They were joined by two slightly larger models in 1970, these being the five-speed CB135 and the four-speed CL135. Both used the same engine bored to 46 mm and 136·3 cc and mirrored the 125s as regards engine and chassis construction. With them came the SL175, which was more of a trail machine than the CL. To this end it sported a short, sprung front mudguard, abbreviated rear guard and an exhaust that ran under the engine, protected by a bash plate, and up alongside the left rear subframe stay. Its front mudguard also went on to the CL175, which retained its usual exhaust system. That same year the 175 cc models switched to the near vertical cylinders and tubular cradle frame that had become common for nearly all the twins. The final new model for that year was the SL350 and this followed the same lines as the 175 except that the exhaust was only slightly angled up. Both it and the 175 had them black finished with chrome heat guards.

Yet another variant came in 1971, this being the GL175, which was built for farming use. To this end it came with a single seat, massive rear carrier, knobbly tyres, sprung mudguards, the CL-type exhaust system and a full chaincase. It looked just the job for the ride down the lane and across the field to repair a fence or check some animals.

The Honda twins had now settled into their pattern for the seventies and had lost the early angular style, the leading link forks and the spine frame. In their place were rather more sedate models that in time were to grow a little too fat for their own good. To help stop them they began to turn to disc front brakes, with the CB450 changing in 1970 and the CB250 and CB350 the following year, although in all cases the drum-braked model was still built.

In 1972 the 125 cc twin appeared with a disc front brake and for this a mechanical operation

Above **Paris Show late 1973 and a CB360, a model that had become a trifle corpulent**

Below **Honda's biggest twin with the longest cam chain, the CB500T of 1975**

was devised with an automatic adjuster. New styling with changes to fuel tank, side covers and mudguards in shape, colour and graphics continued to occur from year to year for all the twins, but the basic range stayed fairly static.

1973 brought the CB200 with either disc or drum front brake and a further extension of bore size of the faithful small twin to 55·5 mm and 198·4 cc. Otherwise it was the mixture as before with twin carburettors and a five-speed gearbox, tubular cradle frame and full equipment. It was joined by the CL200 in 1974, and this represented a final fling for the old-style street scrambler that had in truth been superseded by the trail bikes such as the XL series.

1974 also brought revised medium-range twins in the form of the CB250G and CB360, which had six-speed gearboxes and a good number of internal modifications. The extra capacity of the larger machine came from boring it to 67 mm and 356·8 cc. Outwardly the models continued the style of the older machines and were equipped to the same standards. The larger machine was joined by a street scrambler version, the CL360; this was again in the old style and so really obsolete.

That same year saw the biggest twin become bigger and a full 500. It was renamed the CB500T and the capacity in this case came from increasing the stroke to 64·8 mm, which took it to 498·8 cc. The compression ratio dropped to 8·5:1 and the power also to 42 bhp at 8000 rpm. The engine took the prize for longest cam chain and was to prove more prone to vibration than the 450. The machine itself tended to be overshadowed by the fours on the market and like other firms Honda found out the hard way that public taste had moved away from big vertical twins.

In 1976, the last of what might be termed the Honda twins of the seventies appeared. The last of the old were an attempt to inject some life back into the performance of the mid-range twins and the result was the CJ250T and CJ360T.

Equivalent larger model, the CJ360T with better lines and less stodgy performance than its predecessor

Engine unit and exhausts of the 1976 CJ250 which had lost some weight, also typed the 250T

Weight was cut by reverting to a five-speed gearbox, deleting the electric starter and fitting a two-into-one exhaust on the right. The tank, seat and mudguards were tailored to give a sleeker and lighter look, which did improve the machine appearance, while the handling was better.

Then in 1977 the technology changed, as did the styling. The whole line-up of twins moved forward with the three-valve Dreams in 250 and 400 cc sizes with engine balancer shafts. These revived the Hawk name in the USA, and in the line was an automatic. With the Dreams came a new 125 that ran through its red band to 13,000 rpm, unheard of away from the race track, while in the big class there came the vee twin CX500 with pushrod valve operation and cam chain troubles. Some writers were derogatory, but in the same breath would choose it as one of two dead safe, stone reliable, second-hand buys.

So the Honda twin rolled into the eighties with a line for the times and just as popular as always.

4 | Four—
what a bombshell!

Dateline: October 1968, Tokyo Show, the CB750 engine on display

There is nothing new about the idea of a motorcycle with a four-cylinder engine. Credit for the first goes to Colonel Holden and he built his machine around 1896. A revised version was in production from 1899 to 1902 and these machines had the pistons connected directly to cranks on the rear wheel. They were followed by the Belgian FN, which appeared in 1905 with its in-line engine set along the frame and shaft-drive transmission when most makes still used the belt.

In the USA the Pierce came in 1909 with its frame of very large-diameter tubes, which also formed the fuel and oil tanks, and it too had shaft drive. Fours became popular in America, where the immense distances encouraged the use of large engines and the long wheelbase dictated by the in-line layout gave the owner a comfortable ride.

The Henderson, Ace, Indian and Cleveland were all built in the States, but fours appeared in Europe also. The Danish Nimbus was first built in 1919 and remained in production until 1959 with little change for much of that time. England eschewed the in-line layout, but built fours in other layouts with the Ariel square four, Wooler flat four, which failed to reach production, the Matchless vee four, the AJS vee four and a variety of Brough Superior prototypes. A second and prophetic Ariel four had the engine set along the frame but laid on its side, just as the BMW four that broke their tradition of flat twins in 1983.

From Germany in earlier days came the Zundapp flat four with shaft drive but all-chain gearbox with four sets of sprockets and duplex chains to provide the ratios.

Italy led the way to the transverse, in-line four with its road racing 500s in the postwar era, having used this layout during the 1930s. Protagonists in the early years were OPRA, Rondine, Gilera, Benelli and Bianchi, with Gilera and MV the major runners postwar. Plus Guzzi, of course, who had built a transverse in-line four with the cylinders laid flat in 1930, but then Guzzi would

and did build just about any layout of any number of cylinders up to eight and all in their own unique pattern.

So there was nothing new about a four, it was just that they were only seen on a race track with the exception of the rare man who could afford the highly exotic. There were MVs to be bought, at a price, but for road use riders were stuck with their twins.

Into this picture stepped Honda, with plans to offer machines for the big-bike market. Early reports, late in 1965, spoke of a 650 cc transverse four based on their small car engine but had no real information. At that time the CB450 had just appeared and was nibbling at the competition, but Honda was aware that the cream lay in the larger 650 cc market in America, where biggest

The complete CB750 on show at Tokyo when dreams came true

just had to be best. For that it was no good producing a 500 to outrun the 650s, it had to be bigger and better and to offer all the attractions riders sought.

At that time most big twins were at 650 cc, with the Enfield and Norton at 750 cc. Still in the future were the BSA and Triumph triples and the big Triumph twins. The rumours of a new exotic Honda continued and the English industry began to look nervous, although their sales continued to be good while heavily dependent on the USA market.

In October 1968 at the Tokyo show the blow fell. The CB750 was launched and for the first time a mass-produced four was available. Not only was it a four but it had an overhead camshaft, five gears and a disc front brake, to appeal to the racer in most riders, plus electric start, full equipment and a monster dualseat for the tourers.

The English industry went into disarray. It had already suffered the arrival of the fire-eating Mach III Kawasaki the month before and the sedate-looking but so reliable Suzuki T500 in 1967. The Honda was to prove to be the beginning of the end. It also shattered Kawasaki, who had their own 750 cc four well under development, and inscrutable oriental faces were in great demand while they recovered their breath and went off to produce the Mach IV triple and later the Z1.

The problem the Honda four gave the others was more than its specification; it was its keen price, availability worldwide and its sophistication. Also there was now a generation of riders who had grown up on Hondas, thought Honda and bought Honda knowing they would get a reliable machine with good electrics, no oil leaks and excellent performance.

The machine went on show in Las Vegas in January 1969 and in England in April the same year. Demand was instantaneous and heavy with most of the early production going to the USA. There was never any doubt that the public craved for fours and the CB750 established a trend that was to run for years. The other three Japanese firms were forced to join in until the in-line four became so common it was referred to as the Universal Japanese Motorcycle or UJM and dismissed as so boring that a new layout, the vee four, had to be brought in to stimulate the eighties.

Not so in 1969 when the news broke outside Japan, for excitement was high and the adrenalin flowed. Many refused to believe it at first, even when shown the pictures, and thought it a one-

No need for the number plate, that rear view was enough in 1969

The UK launch of the CB750 was at the Brighton Show in April 1969; the impact was tremendous

off or special build. Then they began to appear on the streets and the numbers grew and grew until LA, London and Paris seemed so full of them you constantly tripped over parked examples.

The heart of the machine was the engine and for a revolutionary unit it was very simple and straightforward. It was well engineered and used common Honda practice in most areas just modified or extended to meet the demands of four cylinders. These ran across the machine and were inclined forward a little with dimensions of 61 × 63 mm, so the capacity was 736·5 cc.

The basis of the engine unit construction was a crankcase split horizontally on the shaft centreline, a separate cylinder block on top of that with the head also a one-piece casting. The crankshaft was a single forging and not pressed together as was usual Honda practice, so the

connecting rods had caps and shells. The main bearings were also shells and there were five in all in housings formed in the case halves.

The rods were forged with the gudgeon pins running directly in them and retained in the pistons with circlips. Each piston was flat topped with small valve cut-aways and produced a compression ratio of 9·0:1. Three rings were fitted, two compression and one oil control, and the pistons moved in a one-piece light alloy block with liners. These protruded from the underside to support the piston and were located at the top with a flange.

The cylinder head was also in light alloy and had two valves per cylinder. They worked in pressed-in guides and each was retained by duplex springs, a collar and split collets. The single camshaft ran direct in four split plain bearings formed as two camshaft holders with four separate top caps. The holders sat on the centre of the cylinder head and were machined as a half bearing at each end. They also extended fore and aft to support the rockers on a total of four pivot pins, each locked in place by a single bolt.

Each pin carried two rockers and each of these had an adjuster at its outer end. Access to these was via eight large round caps in the normal

Honda style all screwed into a one-piece cambox cover. This carried a rev counter drive which meshed with a gear cut on the camshaft and a central separate breather cover held by three screws.

The camshaft was chain driven from a sprocket cut on the centre of the crankshaft. It passed through tunnels cast into the head and barrel with a tensioner set in the back of the latter and a guide roller lower down. The camshaft sprocket was bolted into place and thus the timing was as easy to set as that of a single.

Lubrication was unusual for a Japanese machine in that a dry-sump system was used with the oil tank mounted on the right side of the machine beneath the seat. Otherwise it was a conventional high-pressure arrangement with the pump mounted in the underside of the crankcase with access available by the removal of the finned sump pan. The pump was driven from a

Dry-sump lubrication drawing that shows the mechanical layout of the four to advantage. Note oil feed to rear chain

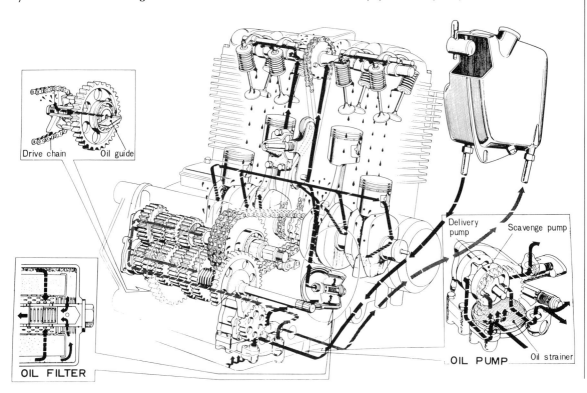

Drive chain   Oil guide

Delivery pump   Scavenge pump

OIL FILTER

OIL PUMP   Oil strainer

gear on the kickstarter shaft and was a double trochoid type with pressure and scavenge rotors.

A valve prevented the oil from draining through the pump and into the sump and pressure was held by a relief valve also in the pump body. The oil went first to a full-flow filter bolted to the front of the crankcase and then to an oil gallery running across the engine behind the crankshaft. The end of this was plugged with a cap that could be changed for a gauge adaptor to allow the oil pressure to be checked.

From the gallery oil went to all five mains and via them to the big ends. Two feeds were taken up barrel studs to lubricate the camshafts and rockers with the surplus draining to the sump. There it was collected by the scavenge pump, itself protected by a gauze strainer, and returned to the oil tank. The scavenge return included a take-off which fed both gearbox shafts and oil was collected in a tray which fed through the output shaft to the final drive sprocket and chain.

Ignition was by two double-ended coils each fired by a contact set. The two sets of points went on a plate under a cover on the right of the crankcase and were opened by a cam on the crankshaft end. Behind it went a centrifugal advance mechanism. An alternator went on the left of the engine and was of the three-phase type with an electromagnetic field coil. Output was controlled by an electromechanical regulator and went via a six-diode rectifier to the 12-volt battery.

The electric starter was a small motor fitted into the top of the crankcase behind the cylinders and masked by a cover plate. It was switched on by a relay and its armature was cut as a pinion which meshed with an idler pair. This passed the drive to a large gear set behind the alternator rotor and this had a roller clutch in its centre.

Four separate 28 mm slide carburettors were used and were located to each other by a plate. Each had its own float chamber and individual settings, but they shared a common fuel supply and all four chokes were linked to a single lever on the left. The four throttle cables ran to a junction box and a single cable went from there to the twistgrip.

The carburettors were connected to the cylinder head inlet stubs by short hoses clamped into place and had a large air cleaner box on the intake side. The lower part of this detached to give access to the filter element within.

On the exhaust side of the engine there were four pipes and four silencers, the first running down from the head together to curl under the engine while, of the latter, the outers ran up at a sharper angle than the inners. It gave the system a magnificent line set off by heat guards bolted to the top silencers.

The pipes were clamped to adaptors which were bolted to the cylinder head and the initial pipe length was double skinned, that is one pipe within another. By this technique, also used on other models, the normal straw and blue heat blemishes common to other machines were eradicated. At their rear ends the silencers on each side were joined by a short tube, but otherwise each system was isolated from the others.

The transmission of the four commenced with two endless chains from the centre of the crankshaft, where two sprockets were cut to the right of the cam chain one. The chains drove back within a chamber to a double sprocket, into which was built a shock absorber. On the lower run a spring-loaded tensioner pulley on an arm kept the chains in check.

The sprocket was fixed to a short hollow shaft that ran on a pair of needle races on the gearbox mainshaft. It ran through one supporting ball race to the clutch drum to which it was splined.

The clutch was a straightforward multi-plate design clamped up by four springs. The ball and ramp lift mechanism went outboard of it and worked through a ball race. It had a screw adjuster within it and the cable ran forward and under the crankcase. A plated cover concealed it and the lever it connected to.

The clutch centre was splined to the gearbox mainshaft and the layshaft lay behind and below it. Both shafts ran in ball races and both carried five pairs of gears to act as an all-indirect box and the ratios were selected by a trio of forks controlled by a barrel cam. This was itself turned by the positive stop mechanism, which went under a cover on the left from which the shaft for the gear lever protruded.

The final drive sprocket was not fitted to either gearbox shaft but to one all of its own that ran in its own bearings right at the rear of the crankcase. It carried a single gear and this meshed with one splined to the layshaft on its extreme right

end, outboard of the gear pairs. The sprocket itself was held in the usual Honda manner with a plate and two small bolts and drove the rear wheel via a heavy-duty chain.

In addition to the electric starter, means of kicking the engine over was provided with a folding pedal on the right side of the machine. The shaft it was fitted to went nearly as far aft as the final drive one, but was set lower in the bottom

Brands Hatch 1969 and Mick Woollett has a run on the CB750 in a show preview

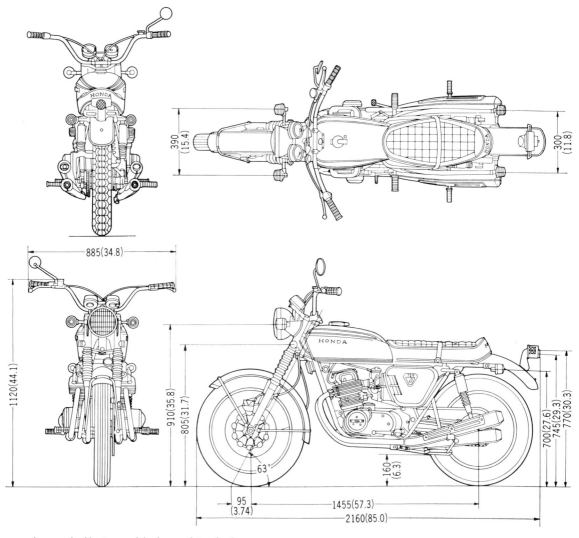

Shape and sizes of the CB750 as given in the 1969 shop manual

crankcase half. Assembled on this shaft was a large gear and a pawl and ratchet mechanism to turn it plus a return spring to hold the pedal at rest. The gear meshed with one fitted to the back of the clutch drum and thus connected to the crankshaft to give primary starting.

The engine with its oil weighed in at 176 lb and produced 67 bhp at 8000 rpm. It was supported in a conventional cradle frame with duplex tubes other than for the top rail. The headstock was heavily braced with pressings as was the rear fork

pivot. The front suspension was by telescopic forks with hydraulic damping, internal springs and gaiters to keep the legs clean. No steering damper was fitted.

The wheels were built up on light alloy hubs with steel rims and wire spokes, while the tyre sizes were 3·25 × 19 in. front and 4·00 × 18 in. rear. The rear brake was the usual Honda single leading shoe type, rod operated by the pedal on the right. At the front went a large-diameter single disc, and in 1968 this was very much a rarity other than on the race track. Operation was hydraulic with the master cylinder at the bars, a joint in the hose lines which included a

Right **Firing up a CB500 four in 1972 for a road test**

Below **Unusual silencer tail shape as found on the 500 alone**

stop-light switch and a hinged caliper with a single working piston.

The mudguards were bright and sporting and the seat long and luxurious with a small upturned tail. It hinged up on one side to give access to the battery beneath it. The fuel tank was equally magnificent in either blue-green or red and was matched by the side panels and air cleaner box.

The seat and tank above the massive engine unit made for a large machine and the bars were to suit. Pillion rests were fitted and also held the silencers in place and the footrests were well back under the nose of the seat. This gave a good riding position, although high, wide and handsome.

Equipment was comprehensive, ranging from good prop and centre stands to a matched pair of large-diameter instruments, back-lit at night, and recording road and engine speeds. The electrical side followed the lines set by the smaller

Above **Clocks and warning light panel used on the fours**

Below **The smallest road four, the CB350 in 1973**

CB750K2 pictured in 1974. Pillion footrests go between the silencers on the 750 only

machines with a full complement of lights and turn signals. The warning lights were set in the instruments with turn and main beam in the speedometer and neutral plus oil pressure in the rev counter.

The switches reflected the period, with the ignition one under the front of the tank and the lights controlled from the right handlebar along with the starter and kill switch. On the left went the turn signal switch and horn button to be joined in later years by a main beam flasher.

The performance was a revelation. Here at last was a quiet, smooth, unobtrusive motorcycle with soft valve timing and wide power band. The five gears were hardly needed but seemed there

more for the sake of image. And it was fast, offering a performance level unheard of for a really mass-produced motorcycle in 1969. There were quicker machines about and ones that were better tourers and others that put the Honda handling to shame in the California canyons or over the bumps and sweeps of the TT Mountain Mile. None combined it all so well as the CB750 and none were so easily available.

The top speed was in the 120 to 125 mph

bracket and the standing quarter time just above 12 seconds. Fuel consumption came out around 50 mpg for most riders with the machine used as a fast tourer and it was as such that the big Honda was best. It became hard work to scratch on it, for the weight and power would become too much for the tyres and handling if pressed too hard. It was best to run the corners at a realistic speed and use the searing acceleration to regain the pace, for even so the machine would give the rider a high average without having to work at it.

The concept of the four was too good to keep to a single model, but before another came the 750 underwent some changes. The first appeared in 1970 as the K0 model, which was built only in very small numbers. The main change was to the carburettor controls, and in place of the four cables went a pair connecting the twistgrip to a drum on a cross shaft. Links and rods joined

this to the throttles and a lighter and smoother system resulted.

It was followed by the K1 in 1971 and this had a number of detail improvements. The chain oiler in the gearbox output shaft received an adjuster and the suspension received some attention, but most changes were cosmetic, with revisions to tank, oil tank, side panels and seat.

Alongside the standard CB750 there arose a flood of special parts to improve both engine and chassis. It was soon demonstrated by the factory that the softly tuned engine could easily be uprated and, more important, was strong enough to withstand the extra loads. So hotter cams, humpy pistons and big-bore kits all made

A classic, the CB400F in 1976. Compact, fast and a good handler, it was very popular

1975 CB400F posed on the beach. The line of the exhaust system was a feature of this model

their appearance. On the chassis side the first steps improved the suspension with roller head races, bushed rear forks, better rear units and European tyres. To this were added fairings and footrests, gas tanks and race seats right through to the complete rolling chassis Rickman built to take the Honda running gear.

The first variation on the four theme was the CB500, which was launched in April 1971. It was based firmly on the larger model as regards layout, but with quite a number of detail changes

inside the covers. Bore and stroke were 56 × 50·6 mm, so the capacity came to 498·5 cc, compression ratio was 9·0:1 and the power 50 bhp at 9000 rpm.

At the top the engine design was changed so that the camshaft ran direct in the cylinder head and the rocker box, with the latter acting as the top cap for the four bearings. It also carried the eight rockers either each on its own shaft or with one shaft shared between each pair.

This made the lubrication even more important and the system was changed to wet sump with the oil in the finned crankcase. This eased the installation problems of the air cleaner, removed two oil pipes and lost one oil pump. The single remaining pump stayed in the trochoid style and was driven from a primary shaft located behind the crankshaft.

The addition of this shaft was not the only change to the transmission, for it was driven from the crankshaft centre by an inverted tooth chain. A gear at the end of the primary shaft meshed with the clutch drum and this went on the gearbox input shaft. The box itself contained five speeds and was of the all-indirect, cross-over type with the final drive on the left. The gear change mechanism went behind the clutch, although the pedal stayed on the left and the clutch lift mechanism was also on that side and operated through the input shaft. All in fact very much as on the twins.

So under the covers there was a revised layout and externally two features set the 500 off from the 750. First was the cylinders, which were vertical and not inclined forward, while second were the ends of the four exhaust pipes, which had a distinctive trumpet form.

Larger version, the CB550F had its own exhaust pipe style to suit the connection to the single silencer

In other ways the CB500 was a repeat of its bigger brother in most details. There were some differences, for it was a smaller motorcycle and its front disc was not so large. The twin instruments were set as on the twins so lacking the style of the 750, while the four warning lights went into a small panel of their own fitted to the handlebars between its clamps. For the rest it was full equipment, lights, controls and fittings as before and a 110 mph performance level.

The same warning light panel appeared on the 750 in 1972 when it became the K2 model and the 500 became the K1. The other changes to the big machine were minor ones and in that form the CB750 ran on in the UK to early 1976. However, there were other variations for the USA with the K3, K4 and K5 following in successive years. For each model there were changes, but these were either cosmetic or minor mechanical improvements.

For the rider who wanted a really smooth four in a smaller size Honda introduced the CB350 in 1972. This was based on the CB500 with the engine dimensions reduced to 47 × 50 mm and the capacity to 347 cc. Compression ratio was 9·3:1 and the power 32 bhp at 9500 rpm. It mimicked the 500 in nearly every way, although there were changes such as the fitting of a smaller rear brake drum. Otherwise it was the same five speeds, electric start, front disc and full equipment. Tyre sizes and gearing were changed to suit the capacity and the small four took its place alongside the twins of the same size.

Both 350 and 500 continued on through 1973 and 1974, at which point the smaller was replaced by a model that was to become a Honda classic, the CB400F. At the same time a replacement for the 500 was introduced, although the older model was continued for 1975 before being withdrawn.

On paper the new 400 was simply the old model bored out to 51 mm and 408 cc. The power was up to 37 bhp at 8500 rpm and the engine followed the same design as the earlier

A CB750F far from home, this was the sports version of the tourer

machines. What set the model off was its sporting appearance, with all four exhaust pipes run into a collector box and single silencer on the right. The sweep of the pipes was sculpted to an exact line so all four came together to run parallel and then back as one.

The rider was provided with six gears in the box to play tunes on, but otherwise the design and layout followed the earlier models. The chassis side also reflected standard Honda thinking, but the revised engine and the tight, light chassis went together to make an excellent machine that quickly became a great favourite and a classic. It was a very sporting motorcycle that handled well, performed well and stopped

well. It was light and easy to throw from side to side in an S bend and the riding position was in the classic European style with narrow bars, the footrests in the right position and a lean-on-the-wind stance.

The second new machine was more sober in appearance and again, on paper, was simply the CB500 bored out to 58·5 mm and 544 cc to become the CB550. In looks it was a dead ringer for the older model, with only the side badges an indication, but on the road it showed that a good few useful changes had been made under the covers. It churned out the same power at a lower engine speed, was very smooth and able to pull from low down. The clutch, gearchange and forks were all modified and the resulting machine was a very fully equipped model that slotted well into the medium-size machine area.

Both the new machines continued in the 1975 range and were joined by two more sports

Above **The left side of this CB750F looks bare without any exhaust pipes**

Below **The CB750K6 model for 1976 with few obvious changes since the launch**

models which took the theme of the 400F into larger sizes. These were the CB550F and CB750F, and the smaller model repeated the style of the 400 with its sensuous exhaust pipes. These lost a little in the translation as they connected into a square form collector and so lost the gracious line of the smallest four.

The remainder of the machine was taken from the stock CB550 but finished in sports style. Detail improvements were a new warning light panel which went between the instruments with the ignition switch below it. This in turn was altered so it also acted as a fork lock, making it simple to turn off the ignition and lock the machine in one move. Also among the electrics was a starter interlock to prevent starting in gear.

The fuel tank was sleeker, with the filler cap hidden beneath a hinged flap in a recess, but the flap lock was no real protection as any blade would turn it. Overall the 550F was longer in the wheelbase than the 400F and not quite so nimble—a touch more determination was

Engine and transmission unit of the CB750A automatic

CB750A instruments with gear indicator and fuel gauge in rev-counter housing

needed to keep it ahead in the curves—but it was faster round a circuit and just as delightful to ride.

The CB750F was a bigger and heavier machine that somehow lacked the neat, even dainty, feel of the small fours. It was an attempt to revive an image that had become tired, for since those heady days of 1968 a good many other superbikes had come on to the market and too many were quicker for Honda's liking.

Hence the F, which had its power pushed back to the 1968 level, from where it had been dragged down by legislation. The appearance was greatly enhanced from the fat tourer image of the original with a new slim fuel tank with recessed cap as on the 550F, new side panels, a seat tail which hid a small luggage box and the expected four-into-one exhaust, albeit without the stylish bends and curves of the smaller machines.

Among the chassis changes were forks without gaiters, a disc brake for the rear wheel and the warning light cluster and ignition switch as on the 550F. Minor changes were also made to the suspension parts and the front brake, while the rear chain became endless to avoid the problem of the weak spring link.

All in all, five fours ran on into 1976 without the CB500. They numbered the 400, two 550s and two 750s. The three F models remained as they were, but the touring 550 became the K2 model, although with little change. The big tourer became the CB750K6 and was built in response to continued demand for the four-pipe

The CB750F2 in 1977 with ComStar wheels and discs front and rear. Two-into-one exhausts on each side

Left **A touring CB550K3 at rest while on test**

Below **As the label says, a CB400F2, not quite as stylish as the original version**

model. It had been intended to replace it with the F model, but plenty of riders still preferred it despite its habit of rusting its silencers from the inside. For the K6 version Honda carried out some minor changes, but one useful one was to increase the size of the bearing behind the gearbox sprocket. On rare occasions the originals had split their outer tracks and caused extensive damage.

There was one further four for 1976 and this represented a radical departure into the realms of automatic transmission. During the seventies the idea of this form of drive seemed an attractive offering to be put before the public on large machines. It already existed for some belt-driven mopeds and the Italian Guzzi marque produced such a model using a torque converter as in a car. In time, though, it was found that even if the automatic could perform better there were few buyers and the inevitable softening of the engine power curve normally pulled the performance down. In the end the makers had to admit that motorcycle customers liked their clutches and manual boxes and so got on with the job of supplying them.

Before that point was reached Honda built the CB750A. This was in design and model form as early as 1973 and was coded the Honda EARA Hondamatic at first. In essence it was the stock engine coupled to a hydraulic torque converter and two-speed gearbox, gear selection being by hydraulic-actuated clutches responding to a foot pedal-controlled selector valve.

The engine was derated with a 7·7:1 compression ratio and smaller carburettors to reduce the power output to 47 bhp at 7500 rpm. The drive was taken from the crankshaft centre to a primary shaft by the usual inverted tooth chain and this in turn drove the torque converter. This assembly was located on to the gearbox input shaft and behind that lay the output shaft carrying the final drive sprocket. Both shafts had two gears and a clutch and these gave the two ratios.

All this transmission swam in the same oil used for the engine and to cope with the job the quantity was increased and the system changed to wet sump. Twin oil pumps remained and the engine side was really unaltered other than for the oil falling into its reservoir. The second pump sent oil direct to the torque converter and not via the filter.

No rev counter was fitted, but its case remained to house large indicators labelled neutral, L and D, which lit up as the ratios were selected. The same housing carried the smaller warning lights and also a fuel gauge of fair accuracy. The speedometer was marked to show that L took the rider from zero to 60 mph while D ran him on to 105 mph.

Safety features included a lockout so that if the side stand was down the transmission could not be moved out of neutral. There was also a parking brake to hold the machine on hills and this held the rear brake on when a knob was pulled.

Right **The last single camshaft four, the CB650 in police guise with special paint, siren and flashing blue lights, the rear one on a telescopic mast**

Below **The standard CB650, overshadowed by the more sophisticated models but a good sturdy machine**

On the chassis side the frame was special to the model with increased trail and longer swinging fork. The tyres were fatter with a 17 in. at the rear and both rims were in light alloy. The exhaust system was a four-into-one as on the F model.

It was an interesting machine and won some fans, but not enough. For 1977 the gearing was revised a little and the exhaust system changed for a four-into-two type with a silencer on each side of the machine. This was not enough to save it and it went from the range in 1978.

1977 saw all the fours continue and the main changes went into the 750s. The sports model became the CB750F2 and received a real

revamp, although it was something of a stopgap pending the arrival of a fresh design. The engine was worked on to push the power up to 73 bhp at 9000 rpm and internally the valves were enlarged and some parts uprated to cope with the added power. Also the engine was finished in black.

For the chassis there were twin discs at the front with the calipers mounted behind the fork legs and of a different design, with single pistons and cross pins to slide on. The wheels were totally new and in the Honda ComStar style they were to use in a variety of forms. In this early type the rim was extruded in aluminium with steel spokes and light alloy hub. The spokes were bolted to the hub and riveted to the rim with plastic mouldings masking the rivet heads. For all the age of its engine the F2 was well able to run with machines which had come much later to the market.

The tourer became the CB750K7 and was fitted with the F1 engine and modified carburettors. The rear chain was altered to a sealed type, so changing it entailed removing the rear fork, and the rear wheel became a 17 in. and the tyre sections as on the automatic.

In the medium range the tourer became the CB550K3 and the sports model the CB550F2, both with minor alterations. The 400 ran on ever popular even in its domestic 399 cc guise. At home there was a limit at 400 cc, above which the rider was subject to far more stringent tests, so few machines were built above that size for home consumption. The top limit was in fact 750 cc, so some of the Japanese industry's most popular big bikes could not be bought by the home population.

The home 400 was just like the export one except that the stroke was reduced to 48·8 mm and the capacity to 398·8 cc. A new barrel with 398 cc cast on to it was used, in fact the same casting with a plate changed in the mould. Power was down one bhp, but it was just as popular in the East as the 400 was in the West.

1978 was the last year for the original single overhead camshaft Honda four. The 750 became the F3 and K8 for the USA market, but with little change, while the smaller sports models became their F2 version. The touring 550 stayed as the K3 and at the end of the year they all went to

Left **Long arms needed on this 12-cylinder drag bike with three well-modified Honda engines**

Below **The Seeley Honda which combined the Japanese engine with an English frame and café racer styling**

be replaced by 400 twins, a 500 vee twin and 750 and 900 cc twin overhead camshaft models.

Later came the fabulous CBX six, a turbo and a range of vee fours, but the old-fashioned in-line four was not altogether forgotten. In 1979 it remained in the line-up as the CB650 and as such represented the logical development of the single-camshaft engine in a chassis and style for the eighties.

The engine was stretched from the 550 to dimensions of 59·8 × 55·8 mm and a capacity of 626·9 cc. Compression ratio was the by now traditional 9·0:1 and power output 63 bhp at 9000 rpm. With a dry weight of 436 lb it was able to offer good performance with a maximum in the 115–120 mph area. Under the covers was the technology of the 550 but upgraded to cope with the extra power and refined in the light of experience. In the manner of the times the exhausts were of the four-into-two type with a silencer on each side.

The frame was modified from the 550 form, although still in the usual Honda four pattern and thus made the machine more stable on the high-way. The chassis was improved with twin front discs, while a drum was retained at the rear to give a combination many riders felt to be the best for road use. ComStar wheels were fitted and the overall styling was in the manner of the new sporting twin-cam models that had joined the range.

The older four thus continued into the eighties, not as a leading light any more but still doing its work and offering the rider a basic, sound model that was fast, flexible and fun to ride. Just as in 1968.

5 | On a Wing or a prayer

A massive motorcycle, the Honda Gold Wing as first seen

Once Honda had launched the CB750 they were faced with two problems. The first was how to make them quickly enough, the second was to wait for the reactions of their rivals. Having dealt with the production problem, they received the answer to the other soon after. Kawasaki already had the H1, which was joined by the 750 cc H2 triple in 1972 to offer raw performance and the Z1 in the same year to give four-cylinder sophistication with added power from 900 cc. Suzuki had the T500 twin and followed this with their water-cooled triple for the fast touring market and later the Wankel-powered RE5 that never really caught on. Yamaha stuck to twins, either hot two-strokes or bigger four-strokes, but also tantalized their competitors by showing their RZ201 with its Wankel engine and a 750 cc road version of their big TZ racer with in-line, four-cylinder, water-cooled engine. Neither of the latter reached the showroom, but by the early seventies Honda knew only too well that their rivals were not idle.

To combat this their first thoughts were to produce one mammoth machine that could be both super sporting and a grand tourer. The result was a prototype with a flat six engine and a capacity of 1·5 litres, bigger than anything else on offer. This was very mildly tuned to produce around 80 bhp and was coupled to a four-speed gearbox with shaft drive to the rear wheel.

In time Honda realized that one machine alone could very easily fall between two stools and so catered for the sporting rider by returning to the in-line, air-cooled engine. This led them to the F series of the 750 model and then to the later twin-cam engines. The climax was still a six, the CBX with its engine set across the frame—so obviously sporting that it set the bureaucrats and ecologists at their rule books to see if it should be banned.

For touring Honda decided to go in another direction and first looked the competition over. The big market was the USA, so the home-grown Harley-Davidson was a strong contender despite its elderly vee twin engine. It was big, strong, fast enough and well used to carrying big American loads over big American distances. It was a tough runner to come up against in a field where sheer performance and nimble handling came well behind the need for sheer grunt.

The other contender they had to fear in the touring market was the German BMW. Although only built in small numbers by Japanese standards the entire production was of high-class, large-capacity machines, so in their class they were significant. BMW flat twins had a charm and character which grew on the rider as the miles went by. At 50 miles one wondered what all the fuss was about, at 500 one knew. It offered comfort, handling, brakes, performance and a big fuel tank. Combined they made 200 miles non-stop normal and easy.

The marque also had its quirks, however. It was essentially a very simple design that had been refined over 50 years and in places this showed. For a start it shook from tick-over to 3000 rpm, though not so much a vibration it was

a shudder that blurred the mirrors. Torque reaction was disconcerting at first, with the machine leaning right as the engine speed rose and left as it dropped.

In the USA the BMW was not used by the out-and-out tourer due to its gross weight limit. In that country touring meant two people, fairing, panniers and top box minimum loaded on to a fully gassed machine—which took it close to its limit even before the luggage was packed. To the majority, touring meant everything including the kitchen sink was taken. For them the flat twin was not the answer.

From this the new touring Honda began to write its specification. It would have a fat rear

Right **Wing bevel box and one exit from the massive silencer**

Far right **Left side of the GL1000 as the Wing was typed**

tyre to take all that weight and the need to shift that weight on grades dictated a large powerful engine. To keep it quiet and cool it would be better if it were water-cooled and to keep it smooth it had to be a four.

The result appeared in 1974 at the Cologne show as the GL1000 Gold Wing and reflected a radical new look in the touring market. The engine was a four, but flat rather than in-line, and was water-cooled with a five-speed gearbox, four carburettors, and shaft drive to the rear wheel. It also had a petrol pump, for the tank was set low beneath the seat—the sheet steel over the engine was a dummy full of air and electrics.

It was a big, heavy, impressive machine, but with the real weight set low to give better than expected handling. It was possibly the most complex engine design for a production motorcycle that the public had ever been let loose on. The later CBX may have looked complex, but once the twin-cam, four-valve concept was accepted it was just more of the same rather than complicated. In contrast the Wing engine unit was at first bewildering with shafts, gears and chains all over the place.

Honda chose to make their new model a one-litre and with engine dimensions of 72 × 61·4 mm the capacity came to just that, a round 1000 cc. Compression ratio was 9·2:1 and power 80 bhp at 7000 rpm. The cylinders were staggered, with

The Gold Wing crankcase
halves with gearbox below
crankshaft and some of
the internal drives

The detachable kickstart
pedal being offered up to
its socket tucked in the
rear of the engine

the right side ahead of the left, although this was
not noticeable due to the arrangement of detail
parts. The crankshaft layout had the front two
pistons moving in opposition to the rear two and
this layout gave complete balance to the primary
and secondary forces in the engine and to the
primary couples. Only the secondary couples
remained and as these were not significant, the

arrangement stayed by virtue of its even firing
interval.

The engine unit assembly included the clutch
and gearbox, the latter being housed beneath
the crankshaft in the massive crankcase castings.
These split on the vertical centreline and each
half extended sideways to include the cylinder
bores and just leave the heads separate. The two

The Wing toothed belt camshaft drives with oil filter and water pump below

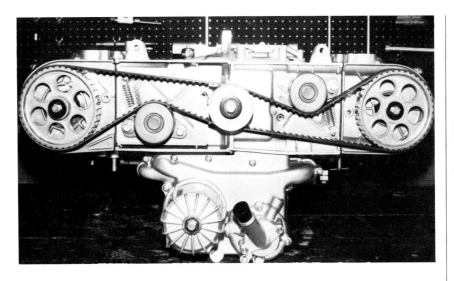

gearbox shafts lay side by side with the input on the centreline and the output on the right-hand side, where it drove the driveshaft which powered the rear wheel.

The crankshaft was forged with three main bearings and a small flywheel at the rear end. It ran in three-shell bearings with an outrigger ball race at the tail—the first was clamped up by caps which bolted to the right case. The big ends were plain shells and the rods steel forgings. The pistons had three rings each, including the scraper, while no circlips were necessary as the gudgeon pins were a force fit.

A single overhead camshaft was fitted to each cylinder head and the drive to them was by toothed Gilmer belts rather than by chain. Each belt was tensioned with a spring-loaded idler wheel and driven by one of the two toothed pulleys fixed to the crankshaft nose. Wheels of twice the diameter went on the ends of the camshafts and the belts were enclosed by the crankcase to the rear and a two-piece cover at the front.

Each camshaft ran in three plain split bearings formed in the head and a rocker support member. The shafts ran directly within the aluminium, which was formed to provide an oil trough for each cam to dip into. These always retained

some lubricant so the wear points never went short even immediately after a cold start. The rocker support was held by the six bolts that clamped the camshaft bearings and it carried the two spindles on which the rockers moved. Each rocker had an adjuster at its outer end and bore on an inclined and offset valve which was controlled by a pair of coil valve springs, both of which were retained by a collar and split collets. A single cover carrying a Honda badge enclosed the whole of the valve gear.

The camshafts each had a dual role and the one on the left 'looked after' the ignition points. Two sets of contacts were mounted on a plate at the rear of the left cambox and each fired two plugs from a double coil. The cam itself was driven via a centrifugal advance unit. A petrol pump at the end of the right camshaft fed the carburettors—necessitated by the low-slung fuel tank beneath the seat which was partly below carburettor level. If the tank was kept about half-full then gravity would be sufficient to feed the carbs, but at any lower level the pump was needed. It was a mechanical unit with a diaphragm moved by a cam-operated lever. This particular cam was formed at the end of the main camshaft and just forward of it went a skew gear which drove the rev counter cable.

The cylinder heads were cast in light alloy with inlets above and exhausts below. The plugs went into angled recesses in the top and the casting was cored for the passage of coolant. Six bolts held each head in place over its two cylinders.

At the rear of the crankshaft there were two gears, the one at the back being meshed with an assembly comprising a double, anti-backlash gear, the alternator rotor and the electric starter

roller clutch. This mass was deliberately rotated in the opposite sense to the crankshaft in order to counteract its torque reaction during acceleration and the reverse. In truth any contra-rotating mass would have done the same job, but rather than employ an otherwise useless lump, Honda chose to make it earn its keep in other ways.

The double gear of this assembly included a cush drive with six rubbers in each gear. A helical

backing spring held them together and damped their movement down. The design took the shock loads off the gear teeth in normal use, but even if the rubbers tore out or were to give under extreme shock loading it was still able to drive.

Just ahead of the gears went a small ball race, while behind them went a larger ball race complete with housing. Behind that came the starter clutch, the centre of which was connected to the motor by a small chain. The motor itself was mounted outside of the crankcase beneath the left cylinder bank. At the rear of the shaft assembly went the alternator rotor held by a single central bolt, while the stator was fitted to the main rear cover.

The second crankshaft gear drove an inverted tooth chain that took the engine power down to the gearbox. The box itself lay ahead of the chain, but the clutch was aft of it in its own sealed chamber—had it been left with the rest of the mechanism it would have been submerged in oil. The gear driven by the primary chain therefore ran free on the mainshaft and was extended through the rear gearbox bearing to carry the clutch.

The clutch itself was a conventional multiplate device with eight friction plates and six springs. Its lift mechanism went into the main rear cover. The gearbox contained five speeds and was of the all-indirect, cross-over type with both input and output shafts supported in ball races. The drive was taken from a sixth gear at the rear of the output shaft and meshed with another gear carried on the drive shaft. This gear was free to turn on the shaft and connected to one half of a cam form damper, the second half of which was splined to the shaft. A hefty coil spring held the two halves together but allowed

some relative movement between them. The complete shaft ran in ball races and a spline at its rear end connected to a universal joint which in turn drove to the rear wheel via a splined joint and bevel gears in the final drive housing.

Although the Gold Wing was a luxury machine aimed at the touring market it was still fitted with a kickstart as a back-up to the electric one. Not that the kickstart was quick or easy to use—the pedal was a separate item that was normally stored in the toolbox and only came out when needed—it was fitted to the rear of the engine and was very much an emergency item.

Yet another drive, this time by duplex chain, was taken from the back of the clutch drum. It descended to the very base of the crankcase, which was the site of two oil pumps and one water pump. These were not all located in one place, however, one oil pump went at the rear of the engine, its sole purpose being to scavenge the clutch chamber and pass any oil it found there back to the sump.

The other oil pump and the water pump went at the front of the engine and were driven from the rear one by a long shaft. Seals kept oil and water apart and both pumps were vented to the atmosphere so that if a leak developed it went outside the engine and did not contaminate the other system.

The lubrication system was of the wet sump variety, the main pump of which collected the oil and passed it to the full-flow filter mounted on the front of the engine. From there the oil went to the mains and big ends, the valve rockers and the primary chain. The connecting rods on the left were drilled to improve cylinder lubrication as the throw of oil from the gearbox favoured the right side of the engine. The oil drained back into the sump with some falling into collector trays and catchment plates from whence it was directed to the point were it could do most good. A gauze filter protected the pump. The final touch was a level window in the side

Under the false Wing tank with the electric components on the left and fuel cap in the centre behind the stowage area

of the engine fitted with its own screwdriver-turned wiper blade.

The water pump bolted to the outside of the engine front alongside the oil filter and was of the normal impeller type. It was part of a sophisticated cooling system with pressurized radiator, remote reservoir, thermostat, temperature gauge and cooling fan. The fan was powered by an electric motor and this was switched by a sensor near the thermostat housing. The all-aluminium engine demanded a suitable anti-freeze and this was used in equal parts with distilled water.

All these above-named revolving parts fitted into the two massive crankcase halves with various covers and lids to keep the oil in, the dirt out and to provide access on demand. It made an impressive lump said to scale 226 lb dry.

On top of the lump went not four carburettors but a hefty assembly of air box, manifolds, linkage mechanisms, control rods, an air cut-off valve, and, nearly as an afterthought, four 32 mm constant-vacuum carbs. With their piston caps shone up and the two curved aluminium intake pipes on each side they set the engine off very nicely. The cut-off valve was used to richen the mixture when the throttle closed, so preventing backfiring, and the butterflies were linked to a common drum with twin cable connection to the twistgrip. A flame trap went in front of each pair of carburettors and a large air cleaner sat above the whole assembly.

The exhaust system commenced with a pair of pipes on each side of the machine which quickly joined together. Each side then connected to a single silencer unit. This gave the impression of being two silencers one on each side of the machine, but in fact the two sides were joined to form one U-shaped chamber wrapped around the rear wheel. At the front of this chamber were the two pipes and at the rear were two outlets, one on each side. The system was coloured black except for the silencer tails, which were chromed, and a similarly finished

heat shield bolted to each silencer side to protect the passenger's feet.

A fully duplex tube frame was used for the Wing, all welded and gusseted to increase its stiffness around the headstock and rear fork pivot. To allow the installation of the engine the bottom left-hand frame rail was detachable, being held by a pair of bolts at each end. The only other special features of the frame were the width across the lower rails, done to straddle the sump, and the whole thing's massive construction.

The rear fork was built up from pressings and moved on needle races. These rode on pivot pins which screwed into housings set in the frame and were adjusted to eliminate any side movement. The drive to the rear wheel passed down the right leg, which was cut short and bolted to the rear bevel box. The drive shaft had a universal joint at its front end, positioned on the fork pivot axis, and various splined members to take up movement and allow a touch of misalignment.

At the front went telescopic forks with internal springs and hydraulic damping but no steering damper. Wire spoke wheels were used with a 3·50 × 19 in. tyre at the front and a 4·50 × 17 in. at the rear. Both had disc brakes and the front had two in acknowledgement of the machine weight. Sliding calipers with a single piston were used and fitted behind the fork legs, while at the rear the light alloy hub had the disc bolted on the left and drive bushes on the right. These engaged with pins set in a spider driven by the crown gear, while the rear caliper had two pistons and was located on to the rear wheel spindle by a single bolt through the left fork leg.

The cosmetic side of the Wing had its unusual points, but not with the mudguards, which were simple chromed sporting ones with the front unsprung and fixed to the fork legs with a stay to the rear. The seat was large with a rail running round behind it and very large side panels went below it on each side to completely fill in the subframe side area. Behind them went the fuel tank, its filler being just ahead of the seat nose. The battery was housed on the left of the seat and the rear brake master cylinder on the right.

Ahead of the seat went what looked like a tank but was in fact a dummy which carried a fuel gauge in its top panel near the front. The gauge was electrically connected to a sender unit with a float in the real petrol tank. At the rear of the dummy's top panel was a lock, the turning of the key in which revealed all. The top hinged up to reveal the filler cap at the rear of the 'tank', a tool compartment and stowage area

for gloves or small parcels. The release of a further catch let the tank sides fall out to the horizontal, in which position they were held by wire cables. The right side concealed the header tank for the cooling system along with the seldom-needed kickstart pedal. To balance it on the left went most of the electrical system, tucked neatly

Not everyone's choice for road racing but better than you might think

Full equipment American style from Custom Dressers of Oklahoma City on a GL1100

in one dry area with plugs and sockets being easily accessible for connecting up.

On the left-hand panel all Wings carried a fuse box, voltage regulator, turn signal relay and temperature gauge regulator, but not the alternator rectifier, which was bolted to the battery carrier. For the USA there was more. The US spec. electrics were trick for 1974; thus, if the dip headlight beam blew the main one came on but at reduced power, and in the same way failure of the tail light brought the stop filament into play at a lower brilliance level. Conversely if the main or stop lights went the dip and tail came on at normal level. A warning light advised the rider

of the changes occurring and resistors on the side panel handled the currents under oscillator and transistor control. For the time these were very sophisticated electronics for a motorcycle.

Finally, on the cosmetics side was the radiator surround which with the dummy tank and side covers gave the machine its colour. Controls were of the normal Honda style, the main instruments being a pair of dials for speedometer and rev counter with the warning lights between them and an ignition key below. The speedo dial included trip and total distance recorders, while the rev counter had the temperature gauge set in it. Warning lights signalled turns, oil pressure, high beam, neutral and, for the USA, the head and tail light tell-tale. There was also a turn signal warning buzzer, but most owners drowned it in a bucket of water.

It added up to 580 lb or so of dry weight, which climbed to around 650 lb when ready for the road. As the gross weight was just over 1000 lb this allowed plenty of latitude for two hefty riders with plenty of their gear packed in the panniers and fairing. As early as the first showing in the USA the Wing was offered with a top fairing and it was to lend itself to accommodating all manner of touring accessories.

The model was quickly nicknamed the Lead Wing as a gibe at its weight, but very soon many thousands found it to be their ideal tourer. It was fast and well able to exceed 100 mph no matter how heavily laden, but really this was totally unimportant. What mattered was its ability to cruise just as fast as the rider wanted it to or at 15 mph with the same ease and stability. The Wing became the supreme tourer and with its low-slung weight was quicker in the curves than many gave it credit for. It was necessary to be firm in an S bend and positive in banking the model from one side to the other, but it responded well. Not a sports bike by any means, but even so it was pretty fast around the TT circuit and as reliable as a stone. Even fuel consumption was not too harsh unless very high cruising speeds were adopted, although even at these 40 mpg was to be expected.

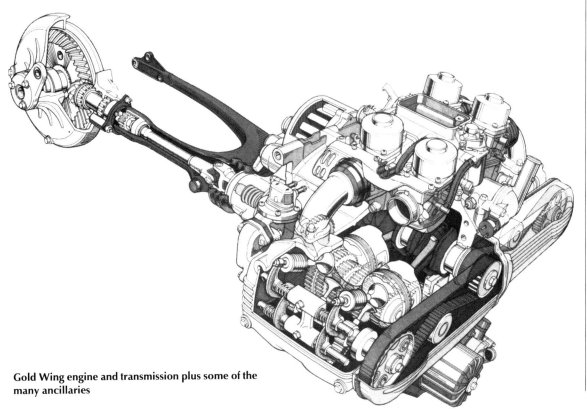

Gold Wing engine and transmission plus some of the many ancillaries

The Wing really was a lovely machine to tour on or to use as a businessman's express. Behind a good fairing a steady 90 mph was no problem and at the end of a journey detachable panniers allowed the papers for a meeting to be taken straight from bike to table. Alternatively the rider could potter along with his luggage in true *gran turismo* style, confident of crossing any country without strain or trouble.

These abilities came from a combination of virtues. The low centre of gravity made the weight relatively easy to handle and the lack of vibration made the machine pleasant to ride. It was long enough to be stable on the highways but not to the point of being unwieldy, for the engine unit, with its transmission underneath the crankshaft, was very compact. The torque reaction problem was avoided by the scheme of running the alternator rotor the opposite way which did balance the forces out. Thus the layout with its crankshaft axis along the machine plus shaft drive did not affect the handling at all.

The ability of the Wing to shift was demonstrated by Fred Chase in November 1976, when he took the Three Flags record in 18 hours and 25 minutes. This was a trip from Cascade, British Columbia, to San Luis in Mexico and over the 1530 miles the Honda averaged 83 mph.

Not much was needed to improve the Wing and it rolled on with mainly cosmetic changes such as the ComStar wheels it eventually gained. Unfortunately emission controls in the USA caused the Wing to suffer from flat spots and slow warm-up. The suspension was something of a problem as the load it had to carry could vary so much. It was stiffened up at one point to stop it bottoming, but then riders complained about the ride quality when out alone and without luggage.

For all that, the Wing proved to be a very popular machine and the tourer's delight. In time it grew to an 1100 and gained front and rear air suspension, which boosted the mid-range power and overcame the variable weight problems.

Honda themselves built a version that came complete with fairing, top box and panniers plus other accessories, and very nice it was too.

In America they were seen in large numbers at rallies, one of the best known of which was the Aspencade. There, Wings with every shape and size of extra would appear and so in time Honda came up with a model of the same name decked out with anything and everything the gadget-conscious tourer could desire. To haul it along the engine was taken up to 1182 cc, but in all other respects it continued as the faithful Wing . . . under all the fittings, that is.

6 | Racers for sale

▶ TOURING STANDARD

Handle Bar ·········Standard type
Sound Arrester ·····Equipped : muffler is used.
Gear Ratio·········   Drive   Driven
                CB 92   15   44
Tire ·············Standard type (Rim type)
Air Pressure ······Front wheel
                   1.8 kg/cm² (25 lb/in²)

Rear Wheel
              2.1 kg/cm² (30 lb/in²)
Spark Plug ······C 7 H or C 8 H
Ignition Timing···5° before upper dead
                           center
Point Gap ······0.3~0.4 mm

▶ HIGHEST SPEED TEST BY FLYING POSTURE

Attention is invited to the fact that for this test an even paved road of approxi-
mately 2,000 m (1-1/4 mile) stretch is required and cannot be done on the
general road.

On account of the driving posture, the center of gravity
becomes high and operation becomes unstable. Be cautious
and examine the road surface carefully.

Handle Bar ············Drop type (genuine part available)
Sound Arrester ·······None, diffuser used.

**Taken from the driver's manual for the CB92 this page
gives the touring settings (top) while the one above
indicates a change of machine settings and riding position
for the quickest run into Tokyo**

The desire to race was seldom dormant in Soichiro Honda for long and led to works teams from the 1950s onwards. This promoted the product and acted as a technical forcing ground and besides he enjoyed it. He was equally aware that many enthusiastic riders were just as keen on racing and that their method of expressing this was through their machine.

Such riders might not be in a position to compete, but in compensation would seek for their machine to be in the racing image. This was nothing new or special to Japan for the business of works replicas for road use was nearly as old as motorcycling itself. Honda was aware of this and realized that there were enough people of that inclination to make such products commercially viable so long as they were based on a production model.

Thus was born the super sporting replica and from that came, on occasion, an out-and-out road racer sold ready for the track.

The first such Honda was the CR71 of 1959, which was based firmly on the CS71 engine unit with its twin cylinders of equal 54 mm dimensions and single overhead camshaft. Its compression ratio was increased to 9·5:1 and the power raised to 24 bhp at 8800 rpm. It retained the four-speed gearbox of the road model, the crankshaft-mounted clutch and its characteristic cable entry and lift mechanism cover. The cycle side was completely changed from the pressed steel of the C and CS machines with a tubular spine frame being used. This followed the same outline, for it had to pick up on the same mountings and its main member ran back from the headstock and then curved down to the rear fork pivot. The main tube was braced with smaller ones and supported a subframe beneath the seat. It was a pattern that was to be repeated more than once.

The front forks remained as leading links with a hefty bracing tube running round behind the wheel to join the two links together. Both wheels had 18 in. rims in place of the standard 16 in. and the front one carried a twin leading shoe brake. The linkage for this was rather messy with the two cams joined by an external rod and the front lever being a bellcrank for the cable connection. This crank stuck out from the hub like a sore thumb, but it gave the required leverage so aesthetics were sacrificed.

At the rear went a single leading shoe drum and tyre sections were 2·75 in. front and 3·00 in. rear. Despite the racing connotations the machine was built for road use and thus came fairly fully equipped. The exhausts terminated in long silencers, one on each side, and a normal dualseat was fitted. Full lighting equipment came with the model and the detail fittings extended to a mirror and a centre stand.

The claimed top speed was about 95 mph and it is likely that were the bike to be reduced to a pure racing form without road items and with megaphone trumpets it would have risen into three figures. Were the rider to add a fairing and a riding position to suit, 110 mph could have been possible. Of course this is no use at all in the 1980s, but in 1959 it was a useful speed for a clubman racer 250 in Europe and elsewhere.

No CR71 models were seen far from home, but in 1960 a close derivative was out and about at the TT. It was a special built for the works riders to use to learn the hard Isle of Man circuit and was therefore fitted out to be road legal. It retained the normal twin-cylinder engine complete with its electric starter and used the spine

The 1959 Formula 1 Honda of 125 cc based on the CB92. Later this model was available with a race kit

frame but was fitted with telescopic front forks. In deference to the law it was equipped with long, shallow taper silencers, lights and a horn. To suit the riders it had clip-ons, rear-sets, remote foot controls and a racing seat, and stood on wheels with alloy rims and single leading shoe drum brakes in full-width, light alloy hubs.

The following year, 1961, the works Hondas made their mark in the 125 and 250 cc classes. To allow the budding club racer to bask in the reflected glory, the firm offered a race kit for the CB92 which, if not converting it into a race winner, would at least give its owner a good ride without him being embarrassed by the machine's speed.

The kit was really quite extensive, for it included pistons, exhaust valves, a camshaft, a new coil, megaphones and a selection of sprockets. Also available were twin Keihin carburettors and a rev counter. The result was a top speed around the 85 mph mark, good brakes and good handling, which in all gave the model acceptable lap times.

Honda's next models for racing were a good deal quicker and a lot more special. There were four of them in total—50, 125, 250, and 305 cc sizes, all twins except the smallest and all using Honda's proven race-winning technology of twin overhead camshafts and four valve heads. They were respectively typed CR110, CR93, CR72 and CR77 and all were listed in Japan in 1962.

The first to be built was the 125 and records indicate that nearly 500 of this model were built of which 30 per cent were pure road racers. The remaining machines were the Dream or rather the Benly, or the café racer, for like the CR71 they came complete with silencers, lights, horn and number plate ready for the road and fully street legal.

The racing CR93 was a classic. It proved to be one of the best production racers of all time, for it was competitive, reliable and pleasant to ride. It was necessary to keep the settings within their limits and to change the oil regularly, but the latter point applied to any Honda on road or track. As a bonus the twin made a lovely noise that would reverberate against the back of the TT grandstand and was lost to the pointless FIM regulations. It was loud, in fact very loud, but lacked the high-pitched whine of the racing two-stroke. Spectators loved it and still do, although extant machines normally only do parades and such like, now.

The engine unit of the CR93 was based on the road machines, but unlike them its dimensions were square at 43 mm so the capacity was

The CB92-derived model that would have run in the 1959 Formula 1 TT except that it was not the required 350 or 500 cc

Above **Road version of the 1962 CR110 with reduced power output but still with eight speeds in the gearbox**

Top **The 1959 CR71 with tubular frame and full road equipment**

124·9 cc. The compression ratio was 10·2:1 and the power output 16·5 bhp at 11,500 rpm. The general construction followed Honda practice except for the camshaft drive, which was all by gears. The crankcase included the gearbox with space for the kickstart at its rear and was horizontally split with the one-piece block on six studs which also held the one-piece head with integral camboxes.

The cylinder head was complex and took as long to set up as the rest of the engine. The parts involved were all rather small, but the actual design was quite straightforward. The casting carried the four valves for each cylinder, in a penthouse form in two parallel pairs. Each tiny valve had a hardened stem tip and was controlled by a pair of coil springs retained by a collar and split collets. Mounted above each pair of valves was a tappet holder fixed with two screws and carrying two tappets. Above them in turn ran the camshaft in two ball races and these were housed in recesses machined in each cambox. They were clamped by a cover held on a total of ten studs and which completed the assembly for each camshaft.

Adjusting the valve clearance was tricky. For a start it could not be measured with the cambox cover in place and without this the camshaft was free to lift away from the tappets. Clamps overcame this, and having checked the gaps to a total variance of three thou the problem was then to correct them if this was needed. The answer was either to surface grind the face to increase the gap or build it up and start again when it became too large.

With that aspect dealt with the budding CR93 racer could move on. The camboxes were sealed on the right by end caps, and the exhaust one carried the rev counter drive. On the left end of the camshafts went the drive gears and the inlet shaft was extended through the end cover to drive the points cam via a centrifugal auto-advance. There were two sets of contacts fitted to the mounting plate, one being allowed relative movement to the other to ensure that both cylinders fired at the correct point. Ignition advance was 52 degrees and the power for the system came from a generator fixed to the left end of the crankshaft.

The two camshaft gears meshed with a single gear set on the cylinder centreline that ran down to the crankshaft. The gear ran on a pair of ball races and these were held on a shaft fitted into the left side of the cylinder head and retained by a single screw.

A cam tunnel was formed in the left of the

Bill Ivy at speed on the 125 cc CR93, a machine he had many successes with

cylinder block and a further gear on two more ball races and a shaft was housed in it, the gear meshing with the one in the head. This was driven by a further idler below it which sat on a pin in the crankcase and meshed with a pinion fitted to the crankshaft inboard of the alternator rotor.

Gaskets went between head, barrel and crankcase with separate seals around the cam drive tunnel.

In the bottom half went a built-up crankshaft with the throws at 180 degrees. All four flywheels were machined round and then grooved near the crankpin to achieve the balance factor. The pins were integral with the inner wheels and the caged needle roller big ends ran direct on them and in the forged rods. Small ends were plain, gudgeon pins held by circlips and the pistons carried a total of three rings.

The crankshaft turned in one ball race main on the right and two roller bearings at centre and left. Location pins held the bearings in place and ensured that the oil supply holes lined up. Lubrication was the typical Honda wet sump with a plunger pump driven by an eccentric on the back of the clutch gear on the gearbox input shaft. A centrifugal oil filter went on the right end of the crankshaft with a breather being sited on top of the crankcase behind the block.

The breather comprised a tower within which was a convoluted passage formed rather like a

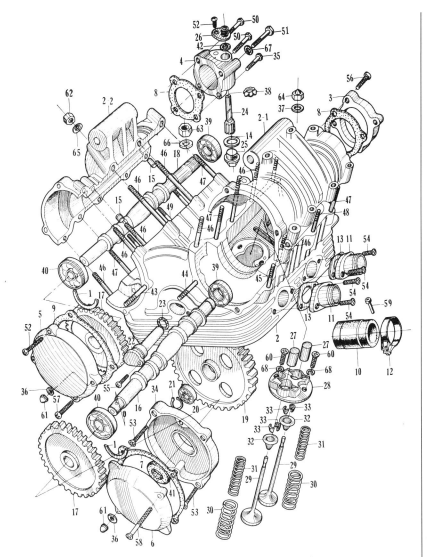

Left **Diminutive Gary Dickinson dwarfed by his CR93 as he pushed off for the 1963 TT. He won a silver replica at over 80 mph**

Left below **The CR93 without its fairing, a classic racing motorcycle**

Right **The CR93 cylinder head and cam boxes as shown in the parts manual**

spiral car park ramp. From the top of the tower a pipe took any escaping oil away. Also set in the top of the crankcase was the detent for the gearchange cam, which rode in the top half above the two shafts and had three selector forks riding on it.

The gearbox was driven by a dry clutch with seven friction and eight plain plates clamped up by six springs. It sat outside the right engine cover

with its own small shield drilled to allow air to reach and cool it. The box itself contained five speeds and was all indirect with cross-over drive and so had the output sprocket on the left. The change mechanism went on the right behind the clutch, but the pedal shaft emerged on the left in the standard Honda style.

On the inlet side of the engine went twin carburettors mounted together as a unit. Each was

fitted with a bell-mouth and was attached by a short rubber hose to a flange bolted to the cylinder head. The carburettors were Keihins with slide throttles and these were lifted by a linkage connected to a drum with push-pull operation by the twistgrip via two cables. Each unit had its own float chamber and these were supplied from a ten-litre aluminium alloy tank with single tap and quick-action filler.

The exhaust side comprised an exhaust pipe welded to a megaphone carried low on each side. The megaphone was long with a shallow taper and a small reverse cone at the end. Caps came with the machine to blank off the outlets and the pipes were held to the ports by sleeve nuts.

The engine was mounted in the frame with the cylinders inclined well forward with the mountings at the rear of the crankcase and the top of the cambox covers because of the tubular

Above **A racing 50 cc CR110 with its fairing**

Right above **Left side of the CR110 showing the much used gear pedal needed to keep the machine in its rev-band**

Right **1962 model CR110 with reversed gear pedal. You need short legs to fit the machine and a light touch to ride it**

spine frame arrangement. This last was built up in the usual Honda manner with a single main tube running from the top of the headstock and curving down behind the engine to the rear fork pivot. Tubes braced the headstock area and others formed the subframe.

At the front went hydraulically damped telescopic forks and these were further controlled by a straight line steering damper. At the rear was a pivoted fork and spring units with oil damping. Both wheels had full-width, light alloy hubs spoked into alloy rims and carried racing tyres of 2·50 × 18 in. front and 2·75 × 18 in. rear. Brakes were drum with a double-sided, single leading shoe at the front and a single-sided one at the rear. Later models were fitted with a single-sided, large-diameter, twin-leading shoe front brake.

A close-fitting front mudguard was used, but at the rear the duty was undertaken by the

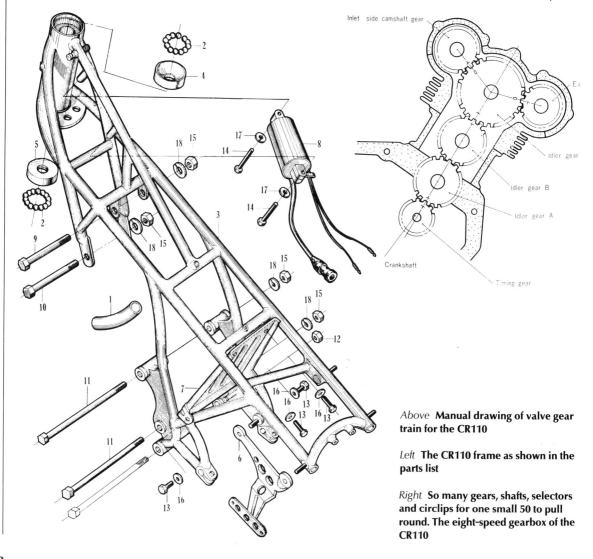

Above **Manual drawing of valve gear train for the CR110**

Left **The CR110 frame as shown in the parts list**

Right **So many gears, shafts, selectors and circlips for one small 50 to pull round. The eight-speed gearbox of the CR110**

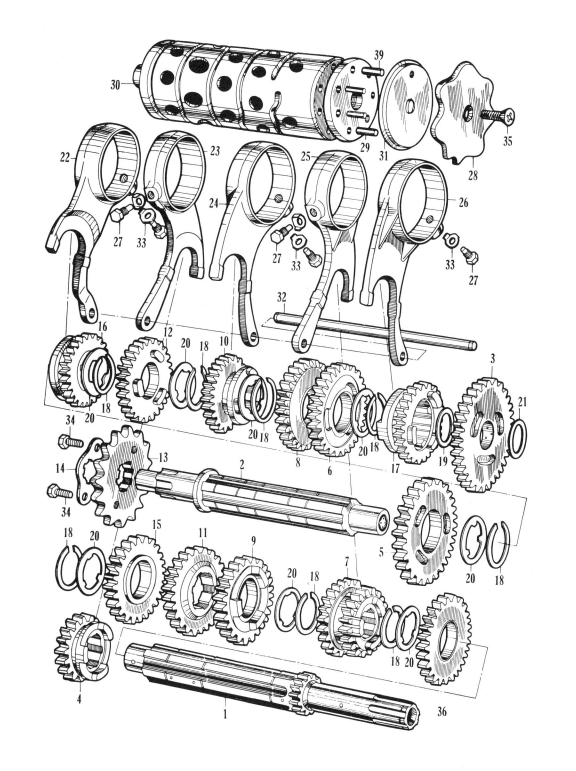

hump-backed seat and a flat plate beneath it to keep stones from entering the bell-mouths. The seat was nicely tailored to look the part and rider comfort was assisted by the footrest mountings. Each rest support was a typical Honda light alloy forging offering a choice of three positions for the rests, although in practice the rear ones were invariably used. At the front went clip-ons with a compensator built into the front brake adjuster to ensure equal pressure on both cam levers.

The rev counter was mechanical and sat ahead of the rider on a stay bolted to the headstock which also carried the front racing plate. Other brackets hung from the seat for the rear plates. Normally the latter were dispensed with and instead an alternative front support which held the dolphin fairing available for the machine was used.

The fairing was constructed from aluminium sheet in two halves with an undertray, screen and front plate. Normally the finish was a delightful silver and orange, which matched in well with the tank, seat and front mudguard. Most models that were supplied with this fairing soon had it changed for a fibreglass one in the interests of preservation.

Finally the fully equipped CR93 racer could buy a Honda tool kit in a case and a Honda stand to support his machine in paddock or workshop.

The machine was a little heavy for a 125 and a little larger than others; nevertheless it was very competitive on the circuits for a number of years and served its riders well. In time it had to give best to the two-strokes in short races,

The CR250 in 1963 as seen at the TT where one model finished third

A superb example of a CR93 complete with fairing. Right gear change and left foot brake on this model

where its bulk told against it, but at the TT it remained successful much longer. On the Mountain circuit its comfort paid off in better riding and its reliability ensured its finishing.

Top speed was around the 100 mph mark on tallish gearing and after a good long run, but in the TT this paid off, for the rider could concentrate on keeping the throttle wide open without the intrusion of cramp. Good brakes helped to stop the not inconsiderable weight and a number of very good riders showed how well the Honda would go round corners.

Maximum power was quoted as coming at 11,500 rpm, but many riders used 13,500 as the red line and if desperate went to 14,500 as an absolute limit, which if used too often proved to be expensive.

The same philosophy applied to the smallest racing model, the 50 cc CR110. This had a single-cylinder engine, but its design and layout followed that of the 125 in many respects. It was inclined further forward and the cambox drive went on the right but remained as a train of spur gears running on ball races and driven by the crankshaft. They were again mounted in crankcase, cylinder tunnel and to the head, but in this case a single cover went on the right side of the cambox to conceal the three gears.

The rev counter continued to be driven by the

exhaust camshaft, but from the left end, where the end cap carried the output shaft. A simple cap went at the left end of the inlet and in other details the 50 was half the 125 with tappet mounting plates on inlet and exhaust sides and camshaft bearings set in the head—the covers that clamped them in place also acting as engine mounts.

When the machine was first seen late in 1961 the contact points were in a housing at the left end of the inlet camshaft as on the twin. Very quickly this arrangement was dispensed with, so the housing became the simple cap described while the points moved to a new housing in the primary drive cover on the right, where the fixed cam sat on its own shaft. This was gear driven from the end of the crankshaft, using the main primary pinion for this purpose, and a generator went on the left end of the crankshaft to provide the power. Some riders were to dispense with the arrangement and use a battery and coil set-up which allowed the engine to rev higher.

The bottom half of the engine was as expected

with the crankshaft built up, a needle roller big end and ball and roller mains. The crankcase was vertically split, but still with the breather tower on top, and was extended to include the gearbox. The gear-driven clutch was dry with four friction and five plain plates clamped by six springs. The pressure plate was formed with a ring of scollops in it to force air through the body of the clutch to cool it.

As on the 125 the lubrication system was a wet-sump one where the oil pump was a single plunger driven off the back of the clutch gear.

The gearbox, after an initial trial with five and then six, eventually contained a total of eight speeds, and was in the normal all-indirect, cross-over form with the output sprocket on the left. A total of five selectors sat on the barrel cam above the two gear shafts and one leg of each was extended to a cross rod along which it slid to be held in alignment. The ratios were as close as those needed by an engine with a small power band.

The carburettor was remotely mounted by

Left **The CR72 which lacks the down tubes of the works CR250 model**

Right **Model used by the works riders in 1960 to learn the TT circuit. Standard C71 engine in modified frame**

hose and at first its slide was lifted by a single cable. This was later changed to a twin push-pull cable connected to a drum linked in the carburettor body to the slide. The exhaust went on the right and was of the short pipe and long, shallow taper megaphone variety favoured by Honda.

On the cycle side it was the CR93 all over again but smaller, shorter, narrower and lighter. The spine frame was however very unusual in its construction for it was fully duplex and based on two tubes running back from the base of the headstock to the rear unit mountings. Braced tubes ran down to support the rear of the engine and the rear fork pivot, while others supported the top of the headstock.

At the front went telescopic forks, at both ends single leading shoe drum brakes in full-width, light alloy hubs. The rims were also light alloy and carried a 2·00 × 18 in. tyre at the front and a 2·25 × 18 in. one at the rear. The control pedals mounted directly to the frame on the CR110 and a kit was available to switch the gear

pedal and footbrake over, this facility also being offered for the CR93.

The seat and tank were narrower and shorter than those of the 125 and the machine came with a rev counter and could be fitted with a fairing.

Fewer 50s were built, but, like the 125, it was offered as a road model. In this form the compression ratio was reduced to 8·5:1 and the power to 7·0 bhp at 12,700 rpm. It kept its eight gears and both tyres became the same section at 2·25 in. On the cycle side it was fitted with a raised exhaust pipe on the right which had a heat shield attached to its silencer. The road equipment was full so Japanese youth could run this near racer with its twin-cam engine and eight gears on the roads with headlamp and the usual fittings which included wider bars and more weight.

The larger twins were both special and rare for only 53 CR72 and 16 CR77s are thought to have been built in all. They followed the well-established CR pattern with gear-driven, twin

overhead camshafts, four valve heads, inclined engine and unit construction. The camshaft drive went between the cylinders, so the block was split vertically to allow assembly of the gears, but the heads were formed in one casting with the camboxes.

In the bottom half of the engine unit went a 180-degree crankshaft, a dry clutch on the left and a six-speed gearbox with the final drive on the right. Engine dimensions remained as for the road models at 54 mm square or 60 × 54 mm and the compression ratio was 10·5:1. Power output was about 41 bhp for the 250 and 47 bhp for the 305, with both engines red-lining at 12,500 rpm and the 305 had more punch so accelerated better as well as being faster.

The cycle side was much as for the 125 with a tubular spine frame, telescopic front forks, straight line steering damper and pivoted rear fork. The machine was fully fitted out for road racing and so came complete with rev counter, race seat, number plates, megaphone exhausts and a lovely noise.

The production CR72 and CR77 were developed from works twins raced at the same period. These were the CR250 and CR305 and looked very similar but were lightened by the use of magnesium castings. The cycle side also dif-

The road-based 750 cc four which won the Bol d'Or in 1969

The 1968 CYB350 based on the road model plus a racing kit

fered as the frame had duplex downtubes and the machines often used the wheels and brakes from the works fours.

After 1967 Honda officially retired from classic racing, but within a year or so had set up the Honda Racing Service Club. This became the source of special parts for racing and gradually the factory became involved again, first at Daytona, then at endurance racing and finally in the classics once more. Before this happened the racing parts became available as race kits and these were sold for both 350 and 750 machines.

The kits were mainly of engine parts with pistons, camshaft, valves, valve springs and car-burettors, but included a more suitable tank, a

Bill Smith giving the four a run at Oulton Park. The machine was based on the CB750 with the race kit added

seat and detail cycle parts. For the 750 it incorporated a new set of rods, a better exhaust system and a set of close-ratio gears.

In addition to the kits there were complete machines. The smaller version was the CYB350, also known as the RSC350, and it was based firmly on the road model with its cradle frame and telescopic front forks. Only 12 were built and the engine was improved to increase its power, and a six-speed gearbox fitted to keep the peaky output on the boil. The cycle parts were modified for road racing with special brakes cast from the works six pattern, so the options for the rider were fairly open—he could buy the machine or use part or the whole of the kit with a road model.

The larger model was the CR750 and this could be created from the road CB750 plus the race kit if this rare item could be found. The engine was remarkably standard, but did have a special crankshaft as well as the better pistons, rods and camshaft. The crank was polished, lightened and carefully assembled and differed from the standard item in that it had a revised end taper for the special ignition generator rotor.

The chassis used the basic road frame minus some brackets and plus some additional ones. The forks at both ends were standard, as was the front wheel, which had twin discs machined thinner to reduce unsprung weight. A massive drum went at the rear with a twin leading shoe brake in it.

Power output was 90 or 96 bhp depending on the camshaft used and the machine was reported to be easy to ride and the engine very flexible. It appeared at a time when road racing in Europe needed a boost and it came via

143

The MT125R, a simple single-cylinder two-stroke with six-speed gearbox

America, 750 Superbikes and later Formula 750.

This led to big, noisy, exciting machines and at first these were all four-strokes. But then came the big two-stroke triples and the very fast TZ350. On many circuits it took an exceptional rider to keep a big, heavy 750 ahead of the nimble Yamaha, so enthusiasm for competition waned. It grew again through the 1970s but instead as a battle for two-strokes until power outputs became so high that the 500 cc grand prix machines lapped faster.

By then the CR750 was long gone and its successors had grown in size to run in open and endurance races with one-litre engines, while Honda produced another production model for road racing. A very different, simple two-stroke of 125 cc, air cooled and with a six-speed gearbox. It was typed the MT125R and was built by what had become known as the Honda Racing Service Centre.

The machines used the motocross engine with detail changes in a straightforward set of cycle parts. In time it became water-cooled, but from the start formed the basis of a successful series of races with Honda promoting the events. It also introduced a sizeable number of machines on to the circuits for the club racer and thus fulfilled one of the basic functions of any production road racing model—keeping the class alive.

It was a far cry from the early CR four-strokes and just not the same thing to listen to. Sitting at the top of the TT grandstand on the Glencrutchery road and listening to a CR93 change down as it pulls in from practice, or (nearly two decades later) to hear an old 305 twin charge off down Bray Hill brought back magic memories of what a racing motorcycle should sound like . . . a four-stroke.

7 | Factory competition

The 250 cc four-cylinder RC160 with its Asama air box and knobbly tyres

Soichiro Honda had raced in pre-war days and so understood why men set out to compete and to prove themselves faster than others. He knew the power of advertising racing successes and how competition could act as a forcing ground for technical advances.

The Japanese industry of the early 1950s was in dire need of technical forcing, for then the machines lagged far behind the best of Europe. There were many Japanese makes, but it was the English or American machines that were wanted in Japan. From this, in time, came the tariffs to protect the industry and then the internal war for survival began.

Part of that war was competition and in Japan this was run for Japanese machines only to promote new ideas and push their acceptance. The industry had seen the effect the big vee-twin Harley-Davidson and Indian machines had on their customers when raced and decided such a diet was really too rich for them. They felt that while Japanese machines might be slower it was better for the spectators to see the home product and so the rules said made in Japan without exception, so no English tyres or Italian brakes, it was all made at home.

One of the earliest races that played its part in this development was the Nagoya TT of 1953. The police would not allow a race as such so the event was billed as a parade over a single 146-mile circuit based on the city of Nagoya and miles of unpaved tracks. With the roads as they

Above **The 250 cc four on the Asama circuit in 1959. The reason for the scrambles tyres becomes evident**

Left **The Honda party at Ronaldsway Airport, Isle of Man, for the 1959 TT**

Right **Engine unit of the 125 cc TT Honda with flat-slide Keihin carburettors and magneto driven by inlet camshaft**

then were in Japan it was more of a motocross or enduro event than a road race, but 19 companies each entered a three-man team, among them Honda.

The latter were fortunate that at the start one of the Showa team machines refused to run and a major rival was reduced to two men. The Hondas were Dream E models with the 150 cc engine in a channel frame fitted with telescopic front forks and plunger rear suspension and were good but not quite good enough. A 150 cc overhead camshaft Showa came home first, but a Honda was second and only 18 seconds adrift after over four hours of racing. The second Showa came third a minute later, but without the third member of the team it was Honda who took the important maker's trophy.

In 1954 a works Dream ran in a race in Brazil with little success, but more important was a visit by Honda himself to the TT races. He came away shaken and stirred. Shaken by the sophistication of the winning machines, especially in the smaller classes, and stirred by the exactness of the

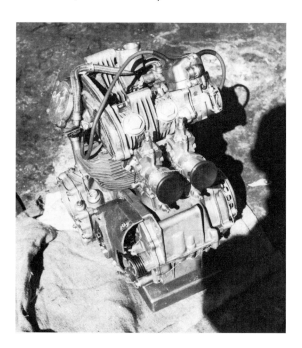

winning NSU models. These German machines had dominated the 250 cc event with only one Guzzi among the first six and were to continue to do so throughout the season. The 125 also won, but was pressed harder by the MV team, although the NSU went on to take the class title that year.

The NSU's teutonic engineering appealed to Honda for they went along the lines he thought were best and there was no denying their success with two world titles in both 1953 and 1954. They followed the basic premise, set out by Dr Lanchester in Edwardian times, that for a given capacity more power came from the use of more and faster cylinders. It was a creed Honda was to adopt and nourish from the start and so the cylinder size came down and the engine speed went up every time they felt they needed more power. To cope with the high crankshaft speed they briefly experimented with desmodromic control, but then turned to the four-valve head.

This last ensured that the tiny valves, always moved by twin overhead camshafts, were light enough to follow the cam form at phenomenal speed and yet remain controllable by springs. It gave a compact combustion chamber with the plug right in the centre, so the flame path was short and direct. Overall the four valves gave better breathing, resulting in greater power.

To Honda, power was all and at times this was their undoing as they moved into the larger classes. More power could and would bring success in the smaller classes, but the large machines needed good handling just as much indeed if not more. Guzzi had proved the point in the 1950s with their ultra-light and well-streamlined 350, while Morini were to follow that path in 1963 with their 250 cc.

Before they achieved their goal, Honda had to become competitive first in Japan and then abroad. In 1954 this was still some way off. After Nagoya there were races at Mount Fuji and the events at Mount Asama. For all its importance in the development of the Japanese motorcycle

Asama was no TT circuit but an unpaved track of dirt and gravel that ran across the slopes of the volcanic mountain for 12 miles that first year in 1955.

The Asama meeting was held in November in bitter cold because being in part on public roads the police forbade it until the weather was such that no sane person would dream of being out on the street. The riders of the 81 machines entered could take their chances as not needing police protection from their odd ideas. Odd it may have seemed to the authorities, but nevertheless 19 makers were there and fielded 38 fac-

Above **Front suspension and front brake of the 1959 125 cc Honda with cable run through brake scoop**

Below **The 250 cc four at the 1960 TT, very much changed from the first model but still not good enough**

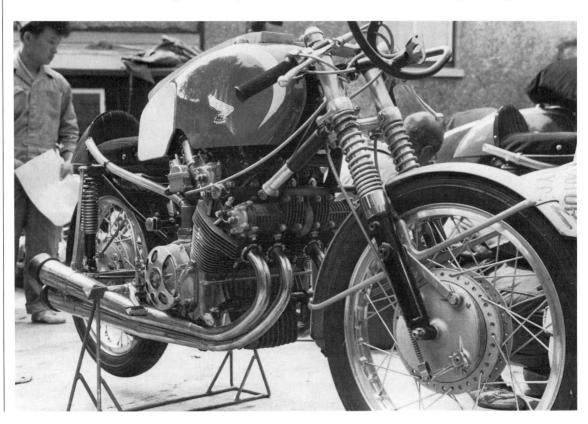

tory road/race machines between them all.

Day one began with a three-lap 125 cc event in which Honda ran tuned JC models which finished well down behind the Yamahas which took the first four places followed by a trio of Suzukis—the best JC was ninth. They did little better in the six-lap 250 cc race, where they fielded five SA-Z machines tuned to give around 18 bhp. Four of these heavy ohc singles fell out and the last came home fourth behind Marusho, Monarch and Pointer machines.

On day two Honda did much better, for they dominated the 350 cc race with their SB-Z Dreams, taking the first five places, while in the 500 cc class a bored-out model came home ahead of the field with DSK, Meguro and Cabton machines hard on its heels. So Honda went home with two wins—which was more than anyone else had achieved. The winning was beginning.

Two years went by before the next race was held and for 1957 a 5·8-mile track was used, still unpaved and mainly surfaced with volcanic ash and gravel. Again Yamaha won the 125 cc race run over 12 laps, but Hondas were third and fourth using the C80Z, a single with gear-driven ohc developing 15 bhp. They had the edge on power but the combination of leading link forks, 18 in. front but 16 in. rear wheels and a doubtful five-speed gearbox combined to pull them back.

The 125 cc RC143 twin-cylinder machine as raced in 1960, much changed from the previous year

Below **Engine unit of the very successful 1961 250 cc four which won ten of the 11 classics**

Above **Bob Brown on the 250 Honda four during the 1960 TT in which he was fourth**

For the 250 cc event Honda used C70Z twins without any success, but their 350 cc C75Z machines and the SB-Z singles came home in the first five places in the 350 cc class once again. In the 500 cc race, run with the 350s, the Meguro singles dominated and so Honda had to make do with only one win.

In 1958 the Asama circuit was used for a club-mans meeting and for the first time amateurs and foreign machines were allowed to compete. In the smaller classes the home machines still hung on, with Yamaha sweeping up the 125 race and

Above **Bob McIntyre setting the 250 cc TT lap record in 1961 before retiring. Mike Hailwood won on a similar Honda four**

Right **Tom Phillis sets out on his last fatal ride on the 284 cc Honda in the 1962 Junior TT. He was their first rider to win a classic**

Honda scraping home in the 250 just ahead of a pair of German Adlers. The bigger class laurels went to England, with a BSA Gold Star winning the 350 and a Triumph the 500. In the final open event Honda ran their 305 cc twins, but again a Triumph won, ridden by American Bill Hunt, who lapped 10 mph faster than the fastest Honda, which came in fourth.

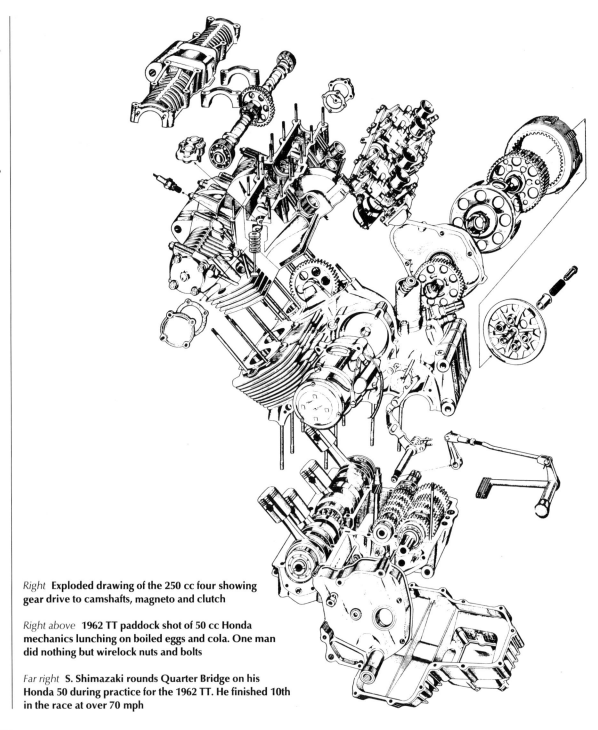

Right Exploded drawing of the 250 cc four showing gear drive to camshafts, magneto and clutch

Right above 1962 TT paddock shot of 50 cc Honda mechanics lunching on boiled eggs and cola. One man did nothing but wirelock nuts and bolts

Far right S. Shimazaki rounds Quarter Bridge on his Honda 50 during practice for the 1962 TT. He finished 10th in the race at over 70 mph

Very soon Hunt was working for Honda and found himself in London early in 1959 to discuss the firm's entry for the 125 cc TT and from there to go on to visit the circuit and make hotel bookings for the races. For their European debut Honda despatched five rides, five race machines, our practice models and spares and tools sufficient for them to set up a self-contained workshop. Honda had decided it was time to run against the best in the world and to subject his machines to the relentless scrutiny of the toughest competition.

The size of the equippe and the cost of its transport halfway round the world alone, showed that they meant business. They came with tyres more suited to the ash of Asama, but soon had racing Avons fitted. The West knew nothing of the Japanese circuit and the knobbly tyres drew more comment than the money Honda was spending on this one event.

The machines were parallel twins, much in the form of the NSU, with the cylinders set near to vertical and twin overhead camshafts driven by a vertical shaft and bevel gears on the left. The magneto was on the right end of the inlet camshaft and the mixture came from flat slide Keihin carburettors fed by remote float chambers. Lubrication was by wet sump with the oil carried in a well-finned sump beneath the crankcase. A

six-speed gearbox was built in unit with the engine and was controlled by a rocking pedal on the left.

The frame was based on a single, large-diameter, curved tube acting as a spine and was bolted to the front of the cambox and the rear of the crankcase. Front suspension was by hefty leading links and at the rear went a pivoted fork. The front brake had a curious appearance, for the operating cable ran through the air scoop to work the linked twin leading shoe cam levers.

The first machines were the two-valve RC141s, but these were not competitive, so four-valve heads were flown from Japan and together with other changes they went to create the RC142. Thus was sown the seed of the Japanese approach with the cost far outweighed by the will to win.

Not that they did any winning in the 1959 TT— the machines were just not fast enough, the handling was doubtful and the riders lacked championship riding experience. In the race Hunt fell, but the other four finished and took the maker's team prize with a best sixth place.

With that gain they showed they had reliability but were some 6 mph off the pace and Honda had spent more on one event than many factories spent on their racing in a year. They returned home to compete in the final Asama races and to plan for 1960, only too aware that they had yet to beat the 125 cc Yamaha at home.

This they did using a team of RC142 models refitted with knobbly tyres suited to the unpaved roads. On the morning of the race they reset their carburettors to suit the conditions, a trick learned in the Island, and went to the line in confident mood. But the factory was not to win—a private C92 Honda slipped ahead to take first place from the three factory RC142s that finished.

If the 125 race had excited the crowds with a sight of the racing Honda twin this was nothing compared with the 250 one that followed it. For

the first time the Honda four was to be seen in public and not one but five machines were unwrapped and warmed up in the pits. For the first time the distinctive howl of the Honda four was heard echoing across the circuit and all turned to listen.

The four was not the first of that size, for both Benelli and Gilera had built such machines, as had a sole English enthusiast, but it was the first to finish in a race. It was in essence a pair of 125 twins on a common crankcase with the camshaft drive still by vertical shaft but on the right. The flat slide Keihin carburettors were fed from an air box protected with fine-gauge gauze and each exhaust carried a megaphone.

Lubrication remained wet sump and the cycle parts were as the 125 with leading link forks and a hump-backed tank. The front brake was from the CR71 and the equipment suited the Asama track. In the race the Hondas, typed the RC160, took the first three places, but for a long period were hard pressed by a private Yamaha twin, which was fair indication that their future opponents would come from Japan, not Europe.

The final day at Asama saw another Yamaha lead a 305 Honda over the line in the 350 cc race and a BMW leading three BSAs in the 500 cc

Above **Engine unit of the 1963 350 four hanging from its spine frame. Gear linkage crosses over to lever low down on left side**

Left above **Jim Redman on the 250 four during the 1963 Tasmanian TT. He won the 125, 250 and 350 events but fell in the 500 chasing for the lead**

Right **The cycle-type rim brake used successfully on the works 50**

Left **The works 50 cc twin, very narrow with wheel discs and high engine speed**

Below **Typical Honda racing four chassis with tubular spine frame and massive drum brakes. This is the 350**

Below right **The power unit of the extraordinary 125 cc Honda 5. When running as here the noise is shattering**

event. Honda went home with two more wins but well aware that they had work to do.

They got down to it and when they went back to Europe for 1960 they took new machines for both the 125 and 250 cc classes. Gone were the upright cylinders, bevel camshaft drive and leading link forks. In their place came inclined engines, central gear drive to the twin camshafts and telescopic forks.

Their first classic was again the TT and again they had to give best to the Italian and East German machines, but managed sixth in the 125 and fourth, fifth and sixth in the 250, with Bob Brown the leading runner. At Assen Jim Redman re-

placed the injured Tom Phillis to take the 125 to fourth and 250 to eighth despite no practice at all on the larger machine.

In Belgium only the 125s ran, well down the field, and then sadly Bob Brown was killed in practice for the West German. This took the pleasure away from Tanaka's third place in the 250 race, but the team cheered up in Ulster, where Phillis and Redman brought their fours home behind the winning MV. Finally at Monza Redman was fourth on the 125 and second on the 250, results that astounded the partisan Italian crowd.

And so to 1961. At the end of 1960 MV effec-

tively withdrew from the smaller classes and their brilliant Carlo Ubbiali retired, while Taveri went to Honda. It was a time of change and Phillis and Redman found that most of the big names were seeking Honda rides. The boss said, 'You rode them when they were slow. You can ride them now they are fast.' And they were and they did.

Honda totally dominated the 125 and 250 cc classics that year, winning eight from eleven in the smaller class and ten from eleven in the larger. Tom Phillis was the first rider to win a classic for them and also took the 125 cc world title. Mike Hailwood won the 250 and at the TT took both classes to give the factory their first Island wins.

The machines and the format was set. Transverse in-line engines, twin overhead camshafts, four-valve heads and smaller and smaller

cylinders. In 1962 they continued to dominate the 125 and 250 cc classes and ventured both up and down in size. Down meant a single-cylinder 50 which only managed one classic win, but the move up gave them a four to run in the 350 cc class, where Redman took the title with four wins in a row. Honda simply took over in 1962. Second in the 350 World Championship was Irishman Tommy Robb with a win in Finland and a second and two thirds. Redman, McIntyre and Phillis were first, second and fourth in the 250 although Robb won the Ulster GP; Taveri, Redman, Robb and Takahashi were first to fourth in the 125; Taveri was third in the 50.

1963 brought more pressure, but Redman retained the 250 and 350 cc titles he had taken in 1962. The 50 again won one race and the 125 three only. Taveri took third in the 350; in the

Left **The 500 cc four of massive power but weak frame that took Hailwood to master it**

Right **The 500 ready to go, a fearsome beast**

Below **Stuart Graham on the 250 cc Honda six during practice for the 1966 TT in which he was second to Mike Hailwood**

Mike Hailwood and Bill Ivy at Brands Hatch in 1967 with the 350 four

250 Robb came third with Taveri fourth; Taveri and Redman, second and third respectively in the 125, built up the numbers. The riders were outstanding, the motorcycles were good too. But for 1964 Honda came back with new models and true to form increased the number of cylinders, pushing engine speeds ever higher.

In the 50 cc class they introduced a twin which ran to close on 20,000 rpm and sometimes used bicycle-type caliper brakes which worked on the wheel rims. It was good but not quite good enough. For the 125 cc class they produced a four and that did better, taking the class titles and TT with Taveri winning both honours. The 350 again swept all before it with Redman winning all eight classics, but in the 250 class it was a different matter altogether.

Throughout the season Redman battled with the Yamaha ridden by Phil Read. Near the end the Honda rider had to win at Monza and for that race they wheeled out a new machine, the RC164 with six cylinders. It was a continuation of the factory theme, and with the RC163 four

near its limit on piston speed the move to a six was natural. In other respects it was much the same as all the previous Hondas but was not to succeed on its debut. Overheating set in and Read won, although the six took the Japanese race at the end of the season with ease.

In 1965 Honda won their first 50 cc title with Ralph Bryans the rider and the machine the twin. The 250 six had problems, for Honda had showed their hand and this led Yamaha to develop their very fast vee four in both 125 and 250 cc sizes. Before it arrived Read had taken the first four classics and this allowed him to keep his title. The 350 was less trouble and Redman retained his crown, although he had to ride hard to keep Agostini and his MV at bay.

The 125 class was a disaster for Honda—the fours had a dreadful year. So much so that a new model was introduced for the Japanese race and this was one of the most unusual of all. Logic said that if the 50 cc twin worked well you used $2\frac{1}{2}$ of them to make a 125. And this is just what Honda did to produce a five-cylinder 125 in their own classic style. The only other odd feature was the exhaust pipe of the centre barrel which would not fit underneath and so ran over the engine and out to the right of the seat.

A 350 Honda four well stripped down during 1967—running repairs maybe

The five nearly had a winning debut, but a broken head bolt slowed it to second place. For 1966 it made no mistake and won its class in a year when Honda took all five solo makers' titles, something never done before, although in earlier times MV had won all four for three years in a row. Hailwood won both 250 and 350 cc titles with ten and six wins respectively using the six- and four-cylinder machines.

The 500 cc title was the one Honda especially sought and for it they fielded a four of considerable power and indifferent handling. At first the class was steered to Redman, but after winning twice he crashed. He never raced again. This left Hailwood with an impossible task—he came very close but was forced out with mechanical trouble in the critical Monza race. Agostini held the rider crown for MV, although Honda did capture the maker's one.

For 1967 they dropped the smaller classes, so the world no longer saw, nor heard, the incredible 125 five or the 50 cc twin. Also unseen was a three-cylinder 50 cc engine built to compete with the similar Suzuki machines. Honda relied heavily on Mike Hailwood that year and placed

A pair of sixes on show at Earls Court in 1967, the year they took both 250 and 350 cc titles

an intolerable burden on his shoulders. It is a measure of his immense ability that he coped with this, and for the 350 cc class rode the six, which was stretched to 297 cc. He won six of the eight events and rated the machine very highly. On the 250 he had Read and Ivy to contend with and a puncture in the first race did nothing to help him. In the end though he took the title by the narrowest of margins from Read, who had ridden so hard all year.

In the 500 cc class it was Mike and the unruly Honda versus Agostini and the handy MV. Only Hailwood's genius kept him ahead in a season

The 1970 Daytona machine based on the CB750 road model

when both riders suffered mechanical failures, with Hailwood retiring more than once when in the lead. Again the title came to depend on Monza and the Honda jammed in top when leading to let the MV past. The points tally was as tight as the 250, but this time it was the other man who came first.

At this point Honda withdrew from grand prix racing. In seven years they had won 16 riders' titles, 18 makers' titles, 18 TTs and 138 grand prix races plus the 1963 350 cc Japanese (which did not count as only three Hondas came to the start line). It was a record anyone could be proud of— the point was made and the name became known worldwide. It was time to cash in on success with the CB750 while the FIM changed the rules and banned many of the exciting and technically advanced Japanese machines.

It was the end of one era and the start of another. Honda kept a low profile for a while, but their road four won the 1969 Bol d'Or and in 1970 the factory ran well-modified CB750s at Daytona. The engines were highly tuned, so veteran Dick Mann geared his machine up and just stayed in touch while his rivals fell by the wayside with various troubles. His was the only Honda to finish, but it was in the place that counts—first by a small margin.

In the early 1970s they became involved with endurance racing and had some success in the production TTs thanks to the efforts of their English dealers. At long-distance events big-bore Honda fours ran and perhaps the best known was the Japauto of around 950 cc. In time it became more and more special with different frame and cycle parts. It was joined by another using an Egli frame and even the Gold Wing formed the basis of one endurance racer.

This rather quiet period ran to 1975, but for the following year Honda came back with big fours with twin-camshaft engines and they dominated the endurance events. They went on with the same basic machines to run in Formula 1 races and in 1977 Phil Read won that

Dick Mann during his winning Daytona ride in 1970. He geared up to stay the course while rivals fell by the wayside

year's TT on an 820 cc four prepared by the factory.

Honda were back in racing in a big way and continued their Formula 1 and endurance racing while they prepared to return to the grand prix with a new 500. It was decreed that being a Honda it had to be a four-stroke, and so was born the NR500 with its radical technology which flourished totally unseen in complete secrecy. From stem to stern the machine was special and very unorthodox—too much so really for it failed to be competitive from its debut in England in 1979.

In the end Honda had to admit that in spite of all the money they were spending the exotic NR was not going to succeed, so they went from the very complex to the simple NS500. This was a very light and compact vee three two-stroke

with reed valves. It ran well in 1982 and then the brilliant Freddie Spencer battled with Kenny Roberts through the 1983 season to take the title by a slim margin.

Honda finally had the 500 cc rider's crown they had striven so hard for.

Appendix

Specifications

Singles

Model	A	B	C	D
Year from	**1947**	**1948**	**1948**	**1949**
No. cylinders	1	1	1	1
Bore (mm)				50
Stroke (mm)				50
Capacity (cc)	50	90	98	98
Compression ratio (to 1)				5·2
Power: bhp		1·2	3	3·5
@ rpm		4500	3000	4500
Valve type	piston	piston	piston	piston
No. gears	1	1	1	2
Final drive	belt	belt	belt	chain
Tyre (in.)		3 wheels	2·50 × 20	3·00 × 20
Front suspension	rigid	girder	girder	teles
Rear suspension	rigid	rigid	rigid	rigid
Ignition system	mag	mag	mag	mag
Wheelbase (in.)			50·4	48·8
Width (in.)			29·1	27·6
Length (in.)			81·5	81·1
Dry weight (lb)			176	176

Model	E	3E	4E	F
Year from	**1951**	**1953**	**1954**	**1952**
No. cylinders	1	1	1	1
Bore (mm)	57	57		40
Stroke (mm)	57	57		40
Capacity (cc)	145	145	220	50
Compression ratio (to 1)	6·5	6·5		5·0
Power: bhp	5·5	5·5	8·5	1·0
@ rpm	5000	5000	5000	3000
Valve type	ohv	ohv	ohv	piston
No. gears	2	3	3	1
Front tyre (in.)	2·75 × 19	2·75 × 19	2·75 × 19	
Rear tyre (in.)	2·75 × 19	2·75 × 19	3·00 × 19	

Model	E	3E	4E	F
Year from	**1951**	**1953**	**1954**	**1952**
Front suspension	teles	teles	teles	
Rear suspension	rigid	plunger	plunger	
Ignition system	mag	mag		mag
Wheelbase (in.)	51·2	51·2	51·2	
Width (in.)	27·6	27·6	29·9	
Length (in.)	83·1	83·1	82·7	
Dry weight (lb)	213	213	312	13·2

Model	J	JA	JB	JC
Year from	**1953**	**1954**	**1955**	**1955**
No. cylinders	1	1	1	1
Bore (mm)		60		
Stroke (mm)		49		
Capacity (cc)	89	138	125	125
Compression ratio (to 1)		6·0		
Power: bhp	3·8	4·5	4·5	7·0
@ rpm	6000	5000	5500	6000
Valve type	ohv	ohv	ohv	ohv
No. gears	3	3	3	4
Tyre (in.)	2·50 × 24	2·50 × 19	2·50 × 24	2·50 × 19
Front suspension	teles	teles	teles	Earles
Rear suspension	s/a	s/a	s/a	s/a
Wheelbase (in.)	47·6	48·4	48·0	49·0
Width (in.)	27·6	29·1	29·5	28·3
Length (in.)	74·0	75·6	74·4	78·0
Dry weight (lb)	209	231	220	242

Model	KB	SA	SB	ME
Year from	**1955**	**1955**	**1955**	**1957**
No. cylinders	1	1	1	1
Bore (mm)	70		76	70
Stroke (mm)	57		76	64
Capacity (cc)	219	246	345	246
Compression ratio (to 1)	6·0			7·5
Power: bhp	9·0	10·5	14·5	14
@ rpm	5500	5000	5400	6000
Valve type	ohv	ohc	ohc	ohc
No. gears	3	4	4	4
Front tyre (in.)	5·00 × 9	2·75 × 19	3·00 × 19	3·00 × 18
Rear tyre (in.)	5·00 × 9	3·00 × 19	3·00 × 19	3·00 × 18
Front suspension	ll	teles	teles	ll
Rear suspension	s/a	s/a	s/a	s/a
Wheelbase (in.)	54·5	53·7	53·7	52·8
Width (in.)	32·3	27·4	27·4	28·5
Length (in.)	81·5	83·7	83·7	81·5
Dry weight (lb)	352	376	383	383

Model	MF	C100	C102	CZ100
Year from	**1957**	**1958**	**1960**	**1960**
No. cylinders	1	1	1	1
Bore (mm)	76	40	40	40
Stroke (mm)	76	39	39	39
Capacity (cc)	345	49	49	49
Compression ratio (to 1)		8·5	8·5	
Power: bhp	20	4·5	4·5	4·5
@ rpm	6500	9500	9500	9500
Valve type	ohc	ohv	ohv	ohv
No. gears	4	3	3	3
Front tyre (in.)	3·00 × 18	2·25 × 17	2·25 × 17	3·50 × 5
Rear tyre (in.)	3·25 × 18	2·25 × 17	2·25 × 17	3·50 × 5
Brake (mm)		110 drum	110 drum	drum
Front suspension	ll	ll	ll	rigid
Rear suspension	s/a	s/a	s/a	rigid
Petrol tank (litre)		3	3	
Ignition system		mag	coil	mag
Wheelbase (in.)	52·8	46·5	46·5	
Width (in.)	28·5	22·6	22·6	
Length (in.)	81·5	70·1	71·2	
Dry weight (lb)	387	143	154	

Model	C110 1	CS50	C50	C320
Year from	**1960**	**1965**	**1966**	**1966**
No. cylinders	1	1	1	1
Bore (mm)	40	39	39	40
Stroke (mm)	39	41·4	41·4	39
Capacity (cc)	49	49·5	49·5	49
Compression ratio (to 1)	9·5	8·8	8·8	
Power : bhp	5·0	5·2	4·8	1·75
@ rpm	9500	10,250	10,000	5750
Torque (kg-m)		0·38	0·37	0·29
@ rpm		9000	8200	3500
Valve type	ohv	ohc	ohc	ohv
No. gears	4 **2**	4	3	4
Front tyre (in.)	2·25 × 17	2·25 × 17	2·25 × 17	
Brake (mm)	110 drum	110 drum	110 drum	
Front suspension	ll	ll	ll	teles
Rear suspension	s/a	s/a	s/a	s/a
Petrol tank (litre)	7	5·5	3	
Ignition system	mag	mag	mag	mag
Wheelbase (in.)	45·3	45·3	46·6	
Width (in.)	22·2	24·2	25·2	
Length (in.)	70·7	69·4	70·7	
Dry weight (lb)	145	168	152	

1 C111 as C110 but single seat, C110D or C114 with low exhaust   **2** early machines—3

Model	P25 1	CL50	SS50	CD50
Year from	**1966**	**1966**	**1967**	**1967**
No. cylinders	1	1	1	1
Bore (mm)	42	39	39	39
Stroke (mm)	35·6	41·4	41·4	41·4
Capacity (cc)	49·3	49·5	49·5	49·5
Compression ratio (to 1)	9·0	9·5	9·5	9·0
Power : bhp	1·2	5·2	6·0	5·2
@ rpm	4200	10,200	11,000	10,250
Torque (kg-m)	0·25	0·385	0·4	0·38
@ rpm	2500	8500	10,000	9000
Valve type	ohc	ohc	ohc	ohc
No. gears	1	4	5 **2**	4
Front tyre (in.)	2·00 × 17 **3**	2·50 × 17	2·50 × 17	2·25 × 17
Rear tyre (in.)	2·25 × 17 **3**	2·50 × 17	2·50 × 17	2·25 × 17
Front brake (mm)			drum **4**	
Front suspension	ll	teles	teles	ll **5**
Rear suspension	rigid	s/a	s/a	s/a
Ignition system	mag			
Wheelbase (in.)	42·1	46·4	46·3	45·3

Model	P25 1	CL50	SS50	CD50
Year from	1966	1966	1967	1967
Width (in.)	24·4	29·1	24·0	24·2
Length (in.)	65·7	70·1	70·5	69·4
Dry weight (lb)	99	152	150	168

1 and P50   **2** with 4 speeds for UK   **3** Dutch P50—19 in. wheels   **4** 1975—disc   **5** 1968—teles

Model	CZ50	C50M	CT50	ST50
Year from	1967	1967	1968	1969
No. cylinders	1	1	1	1
Bore (mm)	39	39	39	39
Stroke (mm)	41·4	41·4	41·4	41·4
Capacity (cc)	49·5	49·5	49·5	49·5
Compression ratio (to 1)	8·8	8·8	8·8	8·8
Power: bhp	2·5	4·8	4·8	4·5
@ rpm	6000	10,000	10,000	9000
Torque (kg-m)	0·31	0·37	0·37	0·37
@ rpm	6500	8000	8200	8000
Valve type	ohc	ohc	ohc	ohc
No. gears	3	3	3 × 2	3
Front tyre (in.)	4·00 × 5 **1**	2·25 × 17	2·25 × 17	3·50 × 10
Rear tyre (in.)	4·00 × 5 **1**	2·25 × 17	2·50 × 17	3·50 × 10
Front suspension	rigid **2**	ll	ll	teles
Rear suspension	rigid	s/a	s/a	s/a
Petrol tank (litre)		3		
Wheelbase (in.)	31·9	46·6	46·8	40·7
Width (in.)	21·5	25·2	28·3	22·8
Length (in.)	45·3	70·7	71·1	58·9
Dry weight (lb)	111	166	157	141

1 1970—3·50 × 8   **2** 1970—teles

Model	PC50	CB50	QA50	PF50
Year from	1969	1971	1971	1971
No. cylinders	1	1	1	1
Bore (mm)	42	42	42	42
Stroke (mm)	35·6	35·6	35·6	35·6
Capacity (cc)	49·3	49·3	49·3	49·3
Compression ratio (to 1)	8·5	9·5	8·5	8·5
Power: bhp	1·8	6·0	1·8	1·8
@ rpm	5700	10,500	5000	5700
Torque (kg-m)	0·29	0·41		0·29
@ rpm	3500	8500		3500
Valve type	ohv	ohc	ohv	ohv
No. gears	1	5	2	1
Front tyre (in.)	2·00 × 19	2·50 × 17		2·00 × 17

Model	PC50	CB50	QA50	PF50
Year from	**1969**	**1971**	**1971**	**1971**
Rear tyre (in.)	2·25 × 19	2·50 × 17		2·00 × 17
Front suspension	ll	teles	teles	teles
Rear suspension	s/a	s/a	rigid	rigid **1**
Petrol tank (litre)				2·3
Wheelbase (in.)	44·5	46·5		42·0
Width (in.)	23·6	26·4		25·0
Length (in.)	69·1	70·1		64·5
Dry weight (lb)	110	163		98 **2**

1 1974—s/a   **2** 1974—107

Model	CF50	CY50	PM50	MR50
Year from	**1972**	**1973**	**1973**	**1974**
No. cylinders	1	1	1	1
Bore (mm)	39	42	40	
Stroke (mm)	41·4	35·6	39·6	
Capacity (cc)	49·5	49·3	49·8	50
Compression ratio (to 1)	8·8		7·5	
Power: bhp	3·5	4·5	1·8	
@ rpm	7500	9500	4000	
Torque (kg-m)	0·37	0·35	0·36	
@ rpm	6000	8000	3000	
Valve type	ohc	ohc	piston	piston
No. gears	3	4	1	3
Tyre (in.)	3·50 × 10	5·40 × 10	2·00 × 17	
Brake (mm)	110 drum			
Front suspension	teles	teles	ll	teles
Rear suspension	s/a	s/a	s/a	s/a
Wheelbase (in.)	43·3	43·9	41·7	
Width (in.)	24·8	30·3	23·8	
Length (in.)	63·6	63·8	65·2	
Dry weight (lb)	152	176	99	

Model	PF50MR	TL50	XE50	C105
Year from	**1975**	**1976**	**1976**	**1961**
No. cylinders	1	1	1	1
Bore (mm)	40	42	42	42
Stroke (mm)	39·6	35·6	35·6	39
Capacity (cc)	49·8	49·3	49·3	54
Compression ratio (to 1)	6·25	9·5	9·5	8·5
Power: bhp	1·93	4·2	4·5	5·0
@ rpm	6000	9500	9000	9500
Torque (kg-m)	0·305	0·36	0·37	
@ rpm	4000	7500	8000	

Model	PF50MR	TL50	XE50	C105
Year from	**1975**	**1976**	**1976**	**1961**
Valve type	piston	ohc	ohc	ohv
No. gears	1	5	4	3
Front tyre (in.)	2·00 × 17	2·50 × 18	2·50 × 16	2·25 × 17
Rear tyre (in.)	2·00 × 17	2·75 × 17	2·75 × 14	2·25 × 17
Front suspension	teles	teles	teles	ll
Rear suspension	s/a	s/a	s/a	s/a
Petrol tank (litre)	2·7			3
Wheelbase (in.)	50·0	46·6	43·5	46·5
Width (in.)	25·0	28·9	27·9	22·6
Length (in.)	66·0	71·8	67·9	70·7
Dry weight (lb)	99	176	172	145

Model	C115	CS65	C65	CL65
Year from	**1961**	**1965**	**1965**	**1968**
No. cylinders	1	1	1	1
Bore (mm)	42	44	44	44
Stroke (mm)	39	41·4	41·4	41·4
Capacity (cc)	54	63	63	63
Compression ratio (to 1)	9·5	8·8	8·8	8·8
Power: bhp	5·0	6·2	5·5	6·2
@ rpm	8500	10,000	9000	10,000
Torque (kg-m)		0·48	0·46	0·48
@ rpm		8500	7000	8500
Valve type	ohv	ohc	ohc	ohc
No. gears	4	4	3	4
Tyre (in.)	2·25 × 17	2·25 × 17	2·25 × 17	2·50 × 17
Brake (mm)		110 drum	110 drum	
Front suspension	ll	ll	ll	teles
Rear suspension	s/a	s/a	s/a	s/a
Petrol tank (litre)		6·5	4·5	
Wheelbase (in.)	43·5	45·3	46·6	46·4
Width (in.)	22·2	24·0	25·2	29·1
Length (in.)	70·7	69·1	70·7	70·1
Dry weight (lb)	145	170	161	156

Model	CD65	C70	ST70	CL70
Year from	**1968**	**1969**	**1969**	**1970**
No. cylinders	1	1	1	1
Bore (mm)	44	47	47	47
Stroke (mm)	41·4	41·4	41·4	41·4
Capacity (cc)	63	71·8	71·8	71·8
Compression ratio (to 1)	8·8	8·8	8·8	8·8
Power: bhp	6·2	6·2	6·0	6·5
@ rpm	10,000	9000	9000	9500

Model	CD65	C70	ST70	CL70
Year from	1968	1969	1969	1970
Torque (kg-m)	0·48	0·53	0·51	0·53
@ rpm	8500	7000	7000	8000
Valve type	ohc	ohc	ohc	ohc
No. gears	4	3	3	4
Tyre (in.)	2·25 × 17	2·25 × 17	3·50 × 10	2·50 × 17
Front suspension	teles	ll	teles	teles
Rear suspension	s/a	s/a	s/a	s/a
Wheelbase (in.)	46·3	46·6	40·7	46·5
Width (in.)	29·9	25·2	22·8	29·7
Length (in.)	71·1	70·7	59·4	70·1
Dry weight (lb)	155	158	143	154

Model	CD70	CT70	CF70	SL70
Year from	1970	1971	1972	1972
No. cylinders	1	1	1	1
Bore (mm)	47	47	47	47
Stroke (mm)	41·4	41·4	41·4	41·4
Capacity (cc)	71·8	71·8	71·8	71·8
Compression ratio (to 1)	8·8	8·8	8·8	8·8
Power: bhp	6·5	6·2	4·5	
@ rpm	9500	9000	7000	
Torque (kg-m)	0·53	0·53	0·53	
@ rpm	8000	7000	5000	
Valve type	ohc	ohc	ohc	ohc
No. gears	4	3	3	4
Front tyre (in.)	2·25 × 17	4·00 × 10	3·50 × 10	2·50 × 16
Rear tyre (in.)	2·25 × 17	4·00 × 10	3·50 × 10	2·75 × 14
Brake (mm)			110 drum	
Front suspension	teles	teles	teles	teles
Rear suspension	s/a	s/a	s/a	s/a
Petrol tank (litre)			2·8	5
Wheelbase (in.)	46·3		43·3	43·3
Width (in.)	29·9		24·8	28·3
Length (in.)	71·1		63·6	67·5
Dry weight (lb)	159		154	143

Model	XL70	ATC70	XR75	XE75
Year from	1974	1974	1973	1976
No. cylinders	1	1	1	1
Bore (mm)	47	47	47	48
Stroke (mm)	41·4	41·4	41·4	41·4
Capacity (cc)	71·8	71·8	71·8	74·9
Compression ratio (to 1)		7·5	8·8	9·0

Honda—The Early Classic Motorcycles

Model	XL70	ATC70	XR75	XE75
Year from	1974	1974	1973	1976
Power: bhp			7·0	6·0
@ rpm			10,000	8000
Torque (kg-m)			0·55	0·57
@ rpm			8500	6000
Valve type	ohc	ohc	ohc	ohc
No. gears		3	4	4
Front tyre (in.)		16 × 8—7	2·50 × 16	2·50 × 16
Rear tyre (in.)		16 × 8—7	3·00 × 14	3·00 × 14
Brake (mm)			110 drum	
Front suspension	teles	rigid	teles	teles
Rear suspension	s/a	rigid	s/a	s/a
Petrol tank (litre)		2·5	4·5	
Wheelbase (in.)		35·2	44·9	43·5
Width (in.)		31·5	29·1	27·9
Length (in.)		51·1	65·7	67·9
Dry weight (lb)		163	141	174

Model	C200	CS90	CM90	CD90
Year from	1963	1964	1965	1965
No. cylinders	1	1	1	1
Bore (mm)	49	50	49	50
Stroke (mm)	46	45·6	46	45·6
Capacity (cc)	86·7	89·5	86·7	89·5
Compression ratio (to 1)	8·0	8·2	8·0	8·2
Power: bhp	6·5	8·0	6·5	7·5
@ rpm	8000	9500	8000	9000
Torque (kg-m)				0·72
@ rpm				6000
Valve type	ohv	ohc	ohv	ohc
No. gears	4		3	4
Tyre (in.)	2·50 × 17	2·50 × 18	2·50 × 17	2·50 × 17
Front brake (mm)	110 drum		110 drum	
Front suspension	ll	teles	ll	ll 1
Rear suspension	s/a	s/a	s/a	s/a
Petrol tank (litre)	8·5		5·5	
Wheelbase (in.)	45·7	47·0		45·3
Width (in.)	24·6	25·6		25·2
Length (in.)	71·1	74·4		70·7
Dry weight (lb)	184	191		187

1 1968—teles

Model	CM91	C90	CL90	CT90
Year from	1966	1966	1966	1967
No. cylinders	1	1	1	1
Bore (mm)	50	50	50	50
Stroke (mm)	45·6	45·6	45·6	45·6
Capacity (cc)	89·5	89·5	89·5	89·5
Compression ratio (to 1)	8·2	8·2	8·2	
Power: bhp	7·5	7·5	8·0	
@ rpm	9500	9500	9500	
Torque (kg-m)	0·67	0·67	0·66	
@ rpm	6000	6000	8000	
Valve type	ohc	ohc	ohc	ohc
No. gears	3	3	4	3 × 2
Front tyre (in.)	2·50 × 17	2·50 × 17	2·50 × 18	
Rear tyre (in.)	2·50 × 17	2·50 × 17	2·75 × 18	
Front suspension	ll	ll	teles	ll
Rear suspension	s/a	s/a	s/a	s/a
Wheelbase (in.)		46·9	47·2	
Width (in.)		25·2	31·9	
Length (in.)		72·0	72·0	
Dry weight (lb)		187	202	

Model	SL90	SL90	CB90	CL90
Year from	1969	1970	1970	1970
No. cylinders	1	1	1	1
Bore (mm)	50	48	48	48
Stroke (mm)	45·6	49·5	49·5	49·5
Capacity (cc)	89·5	89·6	89·6	89·6
Compression ratio (to 1)	8·2	9·5	9·5	9·5
Power: bhp	8·0	9·0	10·5	9·0
@ rpm	9500	9500	10,500	9500
Torque (kg-m)	0·67	0·75	0·76	0·75
@ rpm	8000	7000	9000	7000
Valve type	ohc	ohc	ohc	ohc
No. gears	4	5	5	4
Front tyre (in.)	2·75 × 19	2·75 × 19	2·50 × 18	2·50 × 18
Rear tyre (in.)	3·25 × 17	3·25 × 17	2·50 × 18	2·75 × 18
Front brake			drum **1**	
Front suspension	teles	teles	teles	teles
Rear suspension	s/a	s/a	s/a	s/a
Wheelbase (in.)	48·0	49·4	47·4	47·8
Width (in.)	31·9	31·9	29·5	32·5
Length (in.)	74·0	75·4	74·2	73·6
Dry weight (lb)	216	211	187	205

1 1972—disc

Model	US90 1	ST90	CB100	XL100
Year from	1970	1973	1970	1976
No. cylinders	1	1	1	1
Bore (mm)	50	50	50·5	53
Stroke (mm)	45·6	45·6	49·5	45
Capacity (cc)	89·5	89·5	99·1	99·3
Compression ratio (to 1)	8·2	8·2	9·5	9·4
Power: bhp		6·0	11·5	9·7
@ rpm		8000	11,000	9500
Torque (kg-m)		0·62	0·71	0·75
@ rpm		3500	8000	8000
Valve type	ohc	ohc	ohc	ohc
No. gears	4	4	5	5
Front tyre (in.)	22 × 11—3·5	3·00 × 14	2·50 × 18	2·75 × 19
Rear tyre (in.)	22 × 11—3·5	3·00 × 14	2·50 × 18	3·25 × 17
Front suspension	rigid	teles	teles	teles
Rear suspension	rigid	s/a	s/a	s/a
Petrol tank (litre)				7
Wheelbase (in.)	40·5	45·9	47·4	51·6
Width (in.)	35·4	29·9	29·5	33·1
Length (in.)	62·6	70·1	74·2	80·7
Dry weight (lb)	187	187	192	209

1 later—ATC90

Model	CB125S	CD125S	SL125S	CR125
Year from	1970	1970	1970	1973
No. cylinders	1	1	1	1
Bore (mm)	56	56	56	56
Stroke (mm)	49·5	49·5	49·5	50
Capacity (cc)	121·9	121·9	121·9	123·1
Compression ratio (to 1)	9·5	9·5	9·5	7·6
Power: bhp	12·0	12·0	12·0	21·7
@ rpm	9000	9000	9000	9500
Torque (kg-m)	1·0	1·0	1·0	1·7
@ rpm	8000	8000	8000	9250
Valve type	ohc	ohc	ohc	piston
No. gears	5	4	5	6
Front tyre (in.)	2·75 × 18	2·75 × 18	2·75 × 19	2·75 × 21
Rear tyre (in.)	3·00 × 17	3·00 × 17	3·25 × 17	4·00 × 18
Front suspension	teles	teles	teles	teles
Rear suspension	s/a	s/a	s/a	s/a
Petrol tank (litre)				6
Wheelbase (in.)	47·4	47·2	49·2	53·5
Width (in.)	29·5	32·5	31·9	35·0
Length (in.)	74·8	74·8	75·0	80·3
Dry weight (lb)	194	198	200	178

Model	MT125	TL125	XL125	CG125
Year from	1973	1973	1974	1976
No. cylinders	1	1	1	1
Bore (mm)	56	56	56·5	56·5
Stroke (mm)	50	49·5	49·5	49·5
Capacity (cc)	123·1	121·9	124·1	124·1
Compression ratio (to 1)	6·6	8·0	9·4	9·0
Power: bhp	13·0	8·0	13·0	11·0
@ rpm	7000	8000	9500	9000
Torque (kg-m)	1·4	0·83	1·0	0·94
@ rpm	6500	4000	8500	7500
Valve type	piston	ohc	ohc	ohv
No. gears	5	5	5	4 or 5
Front tyre (in.)	2·75 × 21	2·75 × 21	2·75 × 21	2·50 × 18
Rear tyre (in.)	3·50 × 18	4·00 × 18	3·50 × 18	3·00 × 17 **1**
Front suspension	teles	teles	teles	teles
Rear suspension	s/a	s/a	s/a	s/a
Wheelbase (in.)	53·5	50·4	51·6	47·2
Width (in.)	32·7	33·1	32·7	28·9
Length (in.)	80·9	78·5	82·3	74·8
Dry weight (lb)	211	202	238	207

1 or 2·75 × 18

Model	XL175	MR175	SL250S 1	CR250
Year from	1974	1976	1972	1972
No. cylinders	1	1	1	1
Bore (mm)	64	66	74	70
Stroke (mm)	54	50	57·8	64·4
Capacity (cc)	173·7	171·1	248·6	247·8
Compression ratio (to 1)	9·0	6·8	9·1	7·2
Power: bhp			22	33
@ rpm			8000	7500
Torque (kg-m)			2·0	3·2
@ rpm			6500	6500
Valve type	ohc	piston	ohc	piston
No. gears	5	5	5	5
Front tyre (in.)	2·75 × 21	3·00 × 21	2·75 × 21	3·00 × 21
Rear tyre (in.)	3·50 × 18	3·50 × 18	4·00 × 18	4·00 × 18
Front brake (mm)			160 drum	140 drum
Rear brake (mm)			140 drum	140 drum
Front suspension	teles	teles	teles	teles
Rear suspension	s/a	s/a	s/a	s/a
Petrol tank (litre)	8	10·5	8	7
Ignition system		mag		
Wheelbase (in.)	53·5	54·0	55·1	56·5
Width (in.)	32·5	33·5	29·1 **2**	33·7

Model	XL175	MR175	SL250S 1	CR250
Year from	1974	1976	1972	1972
Length (in.)	81·7	81·0	83·5	83·7
Dry weight (lb)	241	213	279	213

1 1972—XL250   **2** 1973—33·1

Model	MT250	TL250	MR250	XL350
Year from	1973	1975	1976	1974
No. cylinders	1	1	1	1
Bore (mm)	70	74	70	79
Stroke (mm)	64	57·8	64·4	71
Capacity (cc)	246·3	248·6	247·8	348
Compression ratio (to 1)	6·6	9·1	6·9	8·3
Power: bhp	23	16·5		30
@ rpm	6500	7000		7000
Torque (kg-m)	2·6	2·0		
@ rpm	5500	5500		
Valve type	piston	ohc	piston	ohc
No. gears	5	5	5	5
Front tyre (in.)	3·00 × 21	2·75 × 21	3·00 × 21	3·00 × 21
Rear tyre (in.)	4·00 × 18	4·00 × 18	4·00 × 18	4·00 × 18
Front brake (mm)			150 drum	
Rear brake (mm)			140 drum	
Front suspension	teles	teles	teles	teles
Rear suspension	s/a	s/a	s/a	s/a
Petrol tank (litre)		3·6	12·4	8·3
Ignition system			mag	mag
Wheelbase (in.)	56·7	52·2	56·5	55·3
Width (in.)	35·0	33·1	33	34·3
Length (in.)	85·0	80·7		84·3
Dry weight (lb)	260	218	256	321

Twins

Model	C90	C92	CB92	CS92
Year from	1958	1959	1959	1959
No. cylinders	2	2	2	2
Bore (mm)	44	44	44	44
Stroke (mm)	41	41	41	41
Capacity (cc)	124·7	124·7	124·7	124·7
Compression ratio (to 1)	8·5	8·5	10	8·3
Power: bhp	11·5	11·5	15	11·5
@ rpm	9500	9500	10,500	9500

Model	C90	C92	CB92	CS92
Year from	**1958**	**1959**	**1959**	**1959**
Valve type	ohc	ohc	ohc	ohc
No. gears	4	4	4	4
Front tyre (in.)	3·00 × 16	3·00 × 16	2·50 × 18	3·00 × 16
Rear tyre (in.)	3·00 × 16	3·00 × 16	2·75 × 18	3·00 × 16
Front suspension	ll	ll	ll	ll
Rear suspension	s/a	s/a	s/a	s/a
Wheelbase (in.)	49·8	49·8	49·6	49·8
Width (in.)	25·2	25·2	23·4	25·2
Length (in.)	75·2	75·2	73·8	75·2
Dry weight (lb)	253	264	242	264

Model	CB93	M80	CB125	CL125
Year from	**1964**	**1960**	**1966**	**1966**
No. cylinders	2	2	2	2
Bore (mm)	44	43	44	44
Stroke (mm)	41	43	41	41
Capacity (cc)	124·7	124·9	124·7	124·7
Compression ratio (to 1)	9·5	9·0	9·5 **1**	9·0 **1**
Power : bhp	15	11	15	13·5 **2**
@ rpm	10,500	9000	10,500 **3**	10,000
Torque (kg-m)			1·07 **4**	1·08 **5**
@ rpm			9200 **4**	7500 **5**
Valve type	ohc	ohv	ohc	ohc
No. gears	4	variable	4 **6**	4
Front tyre (in.)	2·50 × 18	3·50 × 10	2·50 × 18	2·75 × 18
Rear tyre (in.)	2·75 × 18	3·50 × 10	2·75 × 18	3·00 × 18
Front brake (mm)			drum **7**	
Front suspension	teles	trailing link	teles	teles
Rear suspension	s/a	s/a	s/a	s/a
Wheelbase (in.)	50·3	49·8	50·3	50·0 **8**
Width (in.)	29·3	26·2	29·3	32·7 **9**
Length (in.)	77·7	71·3	77·7 **10**	76·0
Dry weight (lb)	279	321	279 **11**	282 **12**

1 1969—9·4   **2** 1969—14   **3** 1969—11,000   **4** 1969—1·05/9500   **5** 1969—1·06/8500   **6** 1969—5
7 1972—disc   **8** 1969—50·4   **9** 1969—31·9   **10** 1969—77·9   **11** 1969—246   **12** 1969—238

Model	CD125	CS125 **1**	CB135	CL135
Year from	**1966**	**1967**	**1970**	**1970**
No. cylinders	2	2	2	2
Bore (mm)	44	44	46	46
Stroke (mm)	41	41	41	41
Capacity (cc)	124·7	124·7	136·3	136·3
Compression ratio (to 1)	9·0	9·0	9·5	9·5

Model	CD125	CS125 1	CB135	CL135
Year from	**1966**	**1967**	**1970**	**1970**
Power: bhp	12·5	13	15	14
@ rpm	10,000	10,500	11,000	10,000
Torque (kg-m)	0·94	0·95	1·0	
@ rpm	8500	9000	8500	
Valve type	ohc	ohc	ohc	ohc
No. gears	4	4	5	4
Front tyre (in.)	3·00 × 16	3·00 × 16 **2**	2·50 × 18	2·75 × 18
Rear tyre (in.)	3·00 × 16	3·00 × 16 **2**	2·75 × 18	3·00 × 18
Front suspension	teles	teles	teles	teles
Rear suspension	s/a	s/a	s/a	s/a
Wheelbase (in.)	49·2	49·2	50·4	50·4
Width (in.)	28·3 **3**	29·7	28·9	31·9
Length (in.)	73·6 **4**	73·6	77·9	76·0
Dry weight (lb)	253	216	257	246

1 also as SS125   **2** also 2·75 × 17 for SS125   **3** 1969—29·7   **4** 1969—74·4

Model	C95	CB95	CB160	M85
Year from	**1958**	**1958**	**1964**	**1962**
No. cylinders	2	2	2	2
Bore (mm)	49	49	50	50
Stroke (mm)	41	41	41	43
Capacity (cc)	154·6	154·6	161	168·9
Compression ratio (to 1)	8·6	10	8·5	8·5
Power: bhp	13·5	16·5	16·5	12
@ rpm	9500	10,000	10,000	7600
Torque (kg-m)			1·24	
@ rpm			8500	
Valve type	ohc	ohc	ohc	ohv
No. gears	4	4	4	variable
Front tyre (in.)	3·00 × 16	2·50 × 18	2·50 × 18	3·50 × 10
Rear tyre (in.)	3·00 × 16	2·75 × 18	2·75 × 18	3·50 × 10
Front suspension	ll	ll	teles	trailing link
Rear suspension	s/a	s/a	s/a	s/a
Petrol tank (litre)				6
Wheelbase (in.)	49·8	49·2		50·0
Width (in.)	25·2	22·2		26·6
Length (in.)	75·2	74·8		71·6
Dry weight (lb)	264	253		345

Model	CD175	CL175	CB175	SL175
Year from	1967	1967	1968	1970
No. cylinders	2	2	2	2
Bore (mm)	52	52	52	52
Stroke (mm)	41	41	41	41
Capacity (cc)	174·1	174·1	174·1	174·1
Compression ratio (to 1)	9·0		9·1	9·0
Power: bhp	17	20	20	19
@ rpm	10,500	10,000	10,000	9500
Torque (kg-m)	1·29		1·5	1·5
@ rpm	8000		9000	7500
Valve type	ohc	ohc	ohc	ohc
No. gears	4	4	4	5
Front tyre (in.)	3·25 × 16		2·75 × 18	3·00 × 18
Rear tyre (in.)	3·25 × 16		3·00 × 18	3·50 × 18
Front suspension	teles	teles	teles	teles
Rear suspension	s/a	s/a	s/a	s/a
Wheelbase (in.)	49·2	50·3	50·3	51·6
Width (in.)	28·3	31·9	29·3	30·7
Length (in.)	73·6		77·7	78·5
Dry weight (lb)	249	262	264	255

Model	GL175	CB200	CL200	C70
Year from	1971	1973	1974	1957
No. cylinders	2	2	2	2
Bore (mm)	52	55·5	55·5	54
Stroke (mm)	41	41	41	54
Capacity (cc)	174·1	198·4	198·4	247·3
Compression ratio (to 1)	9·5	9·0	9·0	8·2
Power: bhp	19			18
@ rpm	10,000			7400
Torque (kg-m)	1·1			
@ rpm	8000			
Valve type	ohc	ohc	ohc	ohc
No. gears	5	5	5	4
Front tyre (in.)	3·00 × 19	2·75 × 18		3·25 × 16
Rear tyre (in.)	3·00 × 18	3·00 × 18		3·25 × 16
Front brake (mm)		drum or disc		
Front suspension	teles	teles	teles	ll
Rear suspension	s/a	s/a	s/a	s/a
Petrol tank (litre)		9		
Wheelbase (in.)	51·2	50·8		51·6
Width (in.)	32·3	28·3		26·4
Length (in.)	78·3	76·2		78·3
Dry weight (lb)	268	291		348

Model	C71	CS71	RC70f	C72
Year from	**1958**	**1958**	**1958**	**1960**
No. cylinders	2	2	2	2
Bore (mm)	54	54	54	54
Stroke (mm)	54	54	54	54
Capacity (cc)	247·3	247·3	247·3	247·3
Compression ratio (to 1)	8·2	9·0	9·0	8·3
Power: bhp	18	20	20	20
@ rpm	7400	8400	8400	8000
Valve type	ohc	ohc	ohc	ohc
No. gears	4	4	4	4
Front tyre (in.)	3·25 × 16	3·25 × 16	2·75 × 19	3·25 × 16
Rear tyre (in.)	3·25 × 16	3·25 × 16	4·00 × 18	3·25 × 16
Front suspension	ll	ll	Earles	ll
Rear suspension	s/a	s/a	s/a	s/a
Wheelbase (in.)	51·6	51·6	51·6	51·6
Width (in.)	26·4	26·4	32·6	27·0
Length (in.)	78·3	78·3	71·6	78·1
Dry weight (lb)	348	348	319	356

Model	CB72	CS72	CBM72	CL72
Year from	**1960**	**1960**	**1961**	**1962**
No. cylinders	2	2	2	2
Bore (mm)	54	54	54	54
Stroke (mm)	54	54	54	54
Capacity (cc)	247·3	247·3	247·3	247·3
Compression ratio (to 1)	9·5	8·3	9·5	9·5
Power: bhp	24	20	24	24
@ rpm	9000	8000	9000	9000
Valve type	ohc	ohc	ohc	ohc
No. gears	4	4	4	4
Front tyre (in.)	2·75 × 18	3·25 × 16	2·75 × 18	3·00 × 19
Rear tyre (in.)	3·00 × 18	3·25 × 16	3·00 × 18	3·50 × 19
Front suspension	teles	ll	teles	teles
Rear suspension	s/a	s/a	s/a	s/a
Wheelbase (in.)	51·0	51·6	51·0	52·4
Width (in.)	24·2	27·0	29·9	32·1
Length (in.)	79·7	78·1	78·7	78·7
Dry weight (lb)	337	356	343	337

Model	CB250	CL250	CD250	CB250G
Year from	**1968**	**1968**	**1968**	**1974**
No. cylinders	2	2	2	2
Bore (mm)	56	56	56	56
Stroke (mm)	50·6	50·6	50·6	50·6

Model	CB250	CL250	CD250	CB250G
Year from	**1968**	**1968**	**1968**	**1974**
Capacity (cc)	249·3	249·3	249·3	249·3
Compression ratio (to 1)	9·5	9·5	9·5	9·5
Power: bhp	30	27	27	
@ rpm	10,500	10,000	10,000	
Torque (kg-m)	2·14	2·67	2·67	
@ rpm	9500	8000	8000	
Valve type	ohc	ohc	ohc	ohc
No. gears	5	5	4	6
Front tyre (in.)	3·00 × 18	3·00 × 18	3·00 × 18	3·00 × 18
Rear tyre (in.)	3·25 × 18	3·25 × 18	3·25 × 18	3·50 × 18
Front brake (mm)	drum **1**			disc
Front suspension	teles	teles	teles	teles
Rear suspension	s/a	s/a	s/a	s/a
Petrol tank (litre)				11
Wheelbase (in.)	52·0	52·0	52·0	53·0
Width (in.)	30·5	32·7	30·1	31·5
Length (in.)	80·3	78·7	80·3	80·3
Dry weight (lb)	328	326	341	364

1 1971—disc

Model	CJ250T	C75	CS76	C76
Year from	**1976**	**1958**	**1958**	**1960**
No. cylinders	2	2	2	2
Bore (mm)	56	60	60	60
Stroke (mm)	50·6	54	54	54
Capacity (cc)	249·3	305·4	305·4	305·4
Compression ratio (to 1)	9·5	8·2		8·2
Power: bhp	26	21	24	21
@ rpm	9500	7000	8000	7000
Torque (kg-m)	2·0			
@ rpm	8500			
Valve type	ohc	ohc	ohc	ohc
No. gears	5	4	4	4
Front tyre (in.)	3·00 × 18	3·25 × 16	3·25 × 16	3·25 × 16
Rear tyre (in.)	3·50 × 18	3·25 × 16	3·25 × 16	3·25 × 16
Front brake (mm)	disc			
Front suspension	teles	ll	ll	ll
Rear suspension	s/a	s/a	s/a	s/a
Petrol tank (litre)	14			
Wheelbase (in.)	54·1	51·6	51·6	51·6
Width (in.)	27·9	26·4	26·4	26·4
Length (in.)	84·4	78·3	78·3	78·3
Dry weight (lb)	357	337	348	348

Model	C77	C78	CB77	CL77
Year from	**1963**	**1963**	**1963**	**1966**
No. cylinders	2	2	2	2
Bore (mm)	60	60	60	60
Stroke (mm)	54	54	54	54
Capacity (cc)	305·4	305·4	305·4	305·4
Compression ratio (to 1)	8·2	8·2	9·5	9·5
Power: bhp	23	23	28·5	28·5
@ rpm	7500	7500	9000	9000
Torque (kg-m)		2·35		2·44
@ rpm		6000		6500
Valve type	ohc	ohc	ohc	ohc
No. gears	4	4	4	4
Front tyre (in.)	3·25 × 16	3·25 × 16	2·75 × 18	3·00 × 19
Rear tyre (in.)	3·25 × 16	3·25 × 16	3·00 × 18	3·50 × 19
Front suspension	ll	ll	teles	teles
Rear suspension	s/a	s/a	s/a	s/a
Wheelbase (in.)	51·6	51·6	50·8	52·4
Width (in.)	27·0	30·9		32·3
Length (in.)	78·1	77·9	78·7	79·1
Dry weight (lb)	372	372	350	352

Model	CB350	CL350	SL350	CB360
Year from	**1968**	**1968**	**1970**	**1974**
No. cylinders	2	2	2	2
Bore (mm)	64	64	64	67
Stroke (mm)	50·6	50·6	50·6	50·6
Capacity (cc)	325·6	325·6	325·6	356·8
Compression ratio (to 1)	9·5	9·5	9·5	9·3
Power: bhp	36	33	30	
@ rpm	10,500	9500	9500	
Torque (kg-m)	2·55	2·67	2·50	
@ rpm	9500	8000	7500	
Valve type	ohc	ohc	ohc	ohc
No. gears	5	5	5	6
Front tyre (in.)	3·00 × 18	3·00 × 18	3·00 × 19	3·00 × 18
Rear tyre (in.)	3·50 × 18	3·50 × 18	3·50 × 18	3·50 × 18
Front brake (mm)	drum **1**			disc
Front suspension	teles	teles	teles	teles
Rear suspension	s/a	s/a	s/a	s/a
Petrol tank (litre)				11
Wheelbase (in.)	52·0	52·0	52·7	53·0
Width (in.)	30·5	32·7	33·3	31·5
Length (in.)	80·3	82·7	79·7	80·3
Dry weight (lb)	328	326	363	364

1 1971—disc

Model	CJ360T	CB450	CL450	CB500T
Year from	**1976**	**1965**	**1967**	**1974**
No. cylinders	2	2	2	2
Bore (mm)	67	70	70	70
Stroke (mm)	50·6	57·8	57·8	64·8
Capacity (cc)	356·8	444·9	444·9	498·8
Compression ratio (to 1)	9·3	8·5 **1**	9·0	8·5
Power: bhp	34	43 **2**	43	42
@ rpm	9000	8500 **2**	8000	8000
Torque (kg-m)	2·9	3·88 **3**	4·0	3·8
@ rpm	7500	7250 **3**	7000	7000
Valve type	ohc	dohc	dohc	dohc
No. gears	5	4 **4**	4 **4**	5
Front tyre (in.)	3·00 × 18	3·25 × 18	3·25 × 19	3·25 × 19
Rear tyre (in.)	3·50 × 18	3·50 × 18	3·50 × 18	3·75 × 18
Front brake (mm)	disc	drum **5**		disc
Front suspension	teles	teles	teles	teles
Rear suspension	s/a	s/a	s/a	s/a
Petrol tank (litre)	14			16
Wheelbase (in.)	54·1	53·1 **6**		55·5
Width (in.)	27·9	30·7		32·9
Length (in.)	84·4	82·1 **7**		84·6
Dry weight (lb)	357	411		453

1 1968—9·0   **2** 1968—45/9000   **3** from 1968   **4** 1968—5   **5** 1970—disc
6 1968—54·1   **7** 1968—83·3

Fours

Model	CB350	CB400F (Japan)	CB400F (export)	CB500
Year from	**1972**	**1976**	**1974**	**1971**
No. cylinders	4	4	4	4
Bore (mm)	47	51	51	56
Stroke (mm)	50	48·8	50	50·6
Capacity (cc)	347	398·8	408·6	498·5
Compression ratio (to 1)	9·3	9·4	9·4	9·0
Power: bhp	32	36	37	50 **1**
@ rpm	9500	8500	8500	9000
Torque (kg-m)	2·7	3·2	3·2	4·1
@ rpm	8000	7500	7500	7500
Valve type	ohc	ohc	ohc	ohc
No. gears	5	6	6	5
Front tyre (in.)	3·00 × 18	3·00 × 18	3·00 × 18	3·25 × 19 **2**
Rear tyre (in.)	3·50 × 18	3·50 × 18	3·50 × 18	3·50 × 18
Front brake (mm)	disc	disc	disc	260 disc

Model	CB350	CB400F	CB400F	CB500
Year from	**1972**	**1976**	**1974**	**1971**
Rear brake (mm)	160 drum	160 drum	160 drum	180 drum
Front suspension	teles	teles	teles	teles
Rear suspension	s/a	s/a	s/a	s/a
Petrol tank (litre)	12		14	14
Ignition system	coil	coil	coil	coil
Wheelbase (in.)	53·3	53·3	53·3	55·3
Width (in.)	30·7	27·8	27·8	29·3
Length (in.)	81·1	80·3	80·3	83·9
Dry weight (lb)	373	405	375	407

1 1973—48 **2** 1973—18

Model	CB550	CB550F	CB650	CB750
Year from	**1974**	**1975**	**1979**	**1968**
No. cylinders	4	4	4	4
Bore (mm)	58·5	58·5	59·8	61
Stroke (mm)	50·6	50·6	55·8	63
Capacity (cc)	544	544	626·9	736·5
Compression ratio (to 1)	9·0	9·0	9·0	9·0 **1**
Power: bhp	50	50	63	67 **2**
@ rpm	8500	8000	9000	8000 **2**
Torque (kg-m)	4·4	4·2	5·4	6·1 **3**
@ rpm	7500	7500	8000	7000 **3**
Valve type	ohc	ohc	ohc	ohc
No. gears	5	5	5	5
Front tyre (in.)	3·25 × 19	3·25 × 19	3·25 × 19	3·25 × 19 **4**
Rear tyre (in.)	3·75 × 18	3·75 × 18	3·75 × 18	4·00 × 18 **5**
Front brake (mm)	disc	disc	dual disc	296 disc
Rear brake (mm)	180 drum	180 drum	180 drum	180 drum
Front suspension	teles	teles	teles	teles
Rear suspension	s/a	s/a	s/a	s/a
Petrol tank (litre)	14		18	18 **6**
Ignition system	coil	coil	CD1	coil
Wheelbase (in.)	55·3	55·3	56·3	57·3 **7**
Width (in.)	32·7	32·5	30·5	34·8 **8**
Length (in.)	83·1	83·5	86·6	85·0 **9**
Dry weight (lb)	460	423	436	480

1 1977—9·2 **2** 1976—65/8000, 1977—65/8500 **3** 1977—5·9/7500 **4** 1977—3·50 × 19 **5** 1977—4·50 × 17
6 1976—17, 1977—19 **7** 1976—56·7, 1977—58·7 **8** 1976—29·3, 1977—29·9 **9** 1977—89·6

Model	**CB750F**	**CB750F2**	**CB750A**	**GL1000**
Year from	**1975**	**1977**	**1976**	**1974**
No. cylinders	4	4	4	4
Bore (mm)	61	61	61	72
Stroke (mm)	63	63	63	61·4
Capacity (cc)	736·5	736·5	736·5	1000
Compression ratio (to 1)	9·2	9·0	7·7	9·2
Power : bhp	67	73	47	80
@ rpm	8500	9000	7500	7000
Torque (kg-m)	6·1	6·4	5·0	8·0
@ rpm	7500	7500	6000	6500
Valve type	ohc	ohc	ohc	ohc
No. gears	5	5	2 auto	5
Front tyre (in.)	3·25 × 19	3·25 × 19	3·50 × 19	3·50 × 19
Rear tyre (in.)	4·00 × 18	4·00 × 18	4·50 × 17	4·50 × 17
Front brake (mm)	296 disc	dual 276 disc	296 disc	dual 280 disc
Rear brake (mm)	296 disc	296 disc	180 drum	280 disc
Front suspension	teles	teles	teles	teles
Rear suspension	s/a	s/a	s/a	s/a
Petrol tank (litre)	17	18	18	19
Ignition system	coil	coil	coil	coil
Wheelbase (in.)	57·9	58·8	58·1	60·9
Width (in.)	33·9	31·7	33·7	34·4
Length (in.)	86·6	87·2	89·0	90·8
Dry weight (lb)	499			571

Production road racers

Model	**CR71**	**CR110**	**CR93**	**CR72**
Year from	**1959**	**1962**	**1962**	**1962**
No. cylinders	2	1	2	2
Bore (mm)	54	40·4 **1**	43	54
Stroke (mm)	54	39	43	54
Capacity (cc)	247·3	49·99 **2**	124·9	247·3
Compression ratio (to 1)	9·5	10·3 **3**	10·2	10·5
Power : bhp	24	8·5 **4**	16·5	41
@ rpm	8800	13,500 **4**	11,500	12,500
Valve type	ohc	dohc	dohc	dohc
No. gears	4	8	5	6
Front tyre (in.)	2·75 × 18	2·00 × 18 **5**	2·50 × 18	3·00 × 19
Rear tyre (in.)	3·00 × 18	2·25 × 18	2·75 × 18	3·50 × 19
Front brake	drum	drum	dual SLS **8**	dual TLS
Rear brake	drum	drum	drum	drum
Front suspension	ll	teles	teles	teles

Model	CR71	CR110	CR93	CR72
Year from	**1959**	**1962**	**1962**	**1962**
Rear suspension	s/a	s/a	s/a	s/a
Petrol tank (litre)		9·5	10	
Wheelbase (in.)	51·2	45·5	50·2	50·4
Width (in.)	24·4	20·1 **6**	23·6	24·2
Length (in.)	75·6	67·9	77·2	78·7
Dry weight (lb)	297	134 **7**	280	345

Road model CR110—**1** 40   **2** 49·0   **3** 8·5   **4** 7·0/12,700
5 2·25 × 18   **6** 28·5   **7** 165   CR93—**8** or single TLS

Model	CR77	CYB350	CR750	MT125
Year from	**1962**	**1968**	**1970**	**1973**
No. cylinders	2	2	4	1
Bore (mm)	60	64	61	56
Stroke (mm)	54	50·6	63	50
Capacity (cc)	305·4	325·6	736·5	123·1
Compression ratio (to 1)	10·5			
Power: bhp	47		90 or 96	25
@ rpm	12,500			10,500
Valve type	dohc	ohc	ohc	piston
No. gears	6	6	5	6
Front tyre (in.)	3·00 × 19			2·50 × 18
Rear tyre (in.)	3·50 × 19			2·50 × 18
Front brake	dual TLS	drum	dual disc	disc
Rear brake	drum	drum	drum	drum
Front suspension	teles	teles	teles	teles
Rear suspension	s/a	s/a	s/a	s/a
Wheelbase (in.)	50·4			48
Width (in.)	24·2			19·6
Length (in.)	78·7			71
Dry weight (lb)	345			154

2 Model recognition

Honda make it easy to identify any of their machines as the model number forms the prefix to both engine and frame numbers, the first normally with a letter E following the prefix. Confirmation as to the exact year is less easy and would need the use of both engine and frame numbers and the assistance of the local importer.

Machine production was vast and sold all over the world and due to this it is not practical to list the numbers, models and years without producing another book. If the exact year of the machine is needed, reference should be made to the local importer quoting engine and frame numbers. Should the machine have been moved from one country to another further research may be needed.

Colour information of the models is also a problem, but can be obtained in a similar manner. The many alternatives offered, the annual changes, the complex striping plus the differences between one country and the next would take yet another book to detail. The information is best found by consulting the parts book for the model, year and country in question. This will indicate the parts that are finished in colour and, by code, what that colour is.

Model letters

These have been used by Honda since his very first machine and over the years a confusing array has built up. The following is an attempt to put them in order and to give some indication as to what the model is and for what purpose it was built. Suffix letters are not included, but were normally used to indicate model changes, often from year to year but not always. The one exception was for the super sports F series CB models such as the CB400F.

A	first model, clip-on
ATC	all terrain cycle, three wheels
B	second model, bigger clip-on, three wheels
C	third model, bigger engine
C	step-thru
C	basic model in series
CB	sports model
CB . . . F	super sports, four-cylinder model
CBM	high bar sports model
CD	tourer
CF	step-thru with small wheels
CG	basic ohv model
CJ	lighter sports twin, no electric start
CL	street scrambler, early trail model
CM	step-thru
CP	police model
CR	road racing model
CR	motocross model
CS	tourer with raised exhausts
CT	trail version of step-thru
CX	vee twin ohv engine
CY	fun bike with fat balloon tyres
CYB	road racer based on production twin
CZ	monkey bike
D	first Dream
E	first four-stroke
F	rear wheel Cub clip-on
GL	twin built for farm use, trail format
GL	flat four Gold Wing
J	first Benly, much as NSU
K	first scooter, also called Juno
M	scooter with flat twin engine
ME	early 250 cc overhead camshaft single
MF	350 cc version of ME
MR	enduro model
MT	early enduro or serious trail machine
MT	late 125 cc road racing model
P	moped, engine in rear wheel
PC	four-stroke moped
PF	moped, ohv, also called Graduate
PM	two-stroke moped
QA	child's model similar to monkey bike
RC	scrambles model, also a street scrambler
RC	works road racer
SA	first overhead camshaft model, 250 cc
SB	350 cc version of SA
SL	trail model derived from CL
SS	super sports, similar to CB model
ST	miniature model, also called DAX
TL	trials machine
US	first version of ATC range
XE	enduro model with single-cylinder ohc engine
XL	trail model as XE
XR	motocross model as XE
Z	monkey bike

Model charts

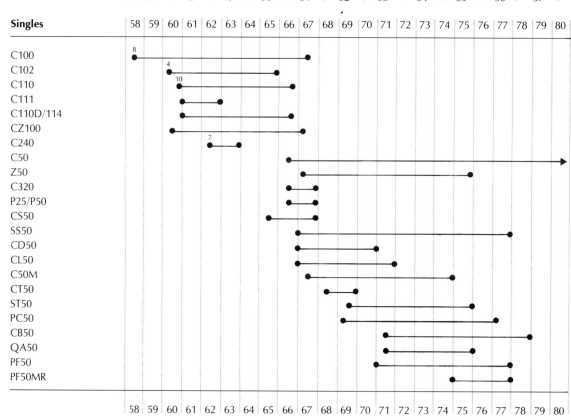

Honda—The Early Classic Motorcycles

188

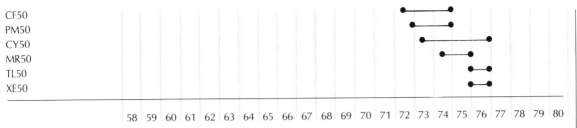

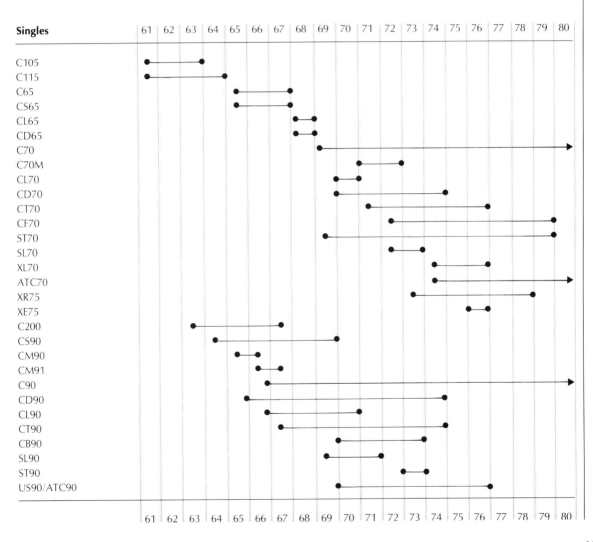

Singles

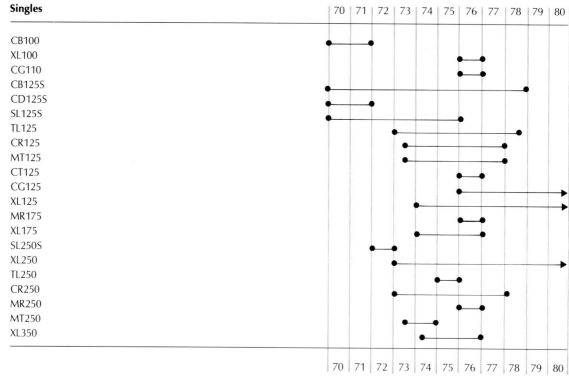

	70	71	72	73	74	75	76	77	78	79	80
CB100											
XL100											
CG110											
CB125S											
CD125S											
SL125S											
TL125											
CR125											
MT125											
CT125											
CG125											
XL125											
MR175											
XL175											
SL250S											
XL250											
TL250											
CR250											
MR250											
MT250											
XL350											

| | 70 | 71 | 72 | 73 | 74 | 75 | 76 | 77 | 78 | 79 | 80 |

Twins

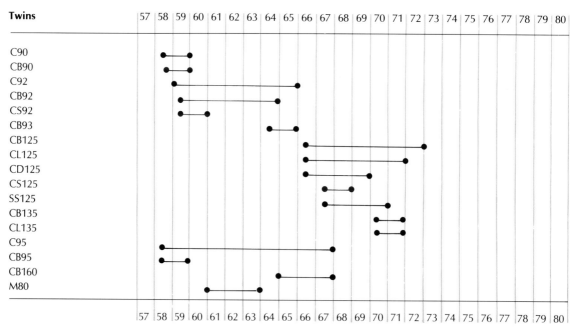

	57	58	59	60	61	62	63	64	65	66	67	68	69	70	71	72	73	74	75	76	77	78	79	80
C90																								
CB90																								
C92																								
CB92																								
CS92																								
CB93																								
CB125																								
CL125																								
CD125																								
CS125																								
SS125																								
CB135																								
CL135																								
C95																								
CB95																								
CB160																								
M80																								

| | 57 | 58 | 59 | 60 | 61 | 62 | 63 | 64 | 65 | 66 | 67 | 68 | 69 | 70 | 71 | 72 | 73 | 74 | 75 | 76 | 77 | 78 | 79 | 80 |

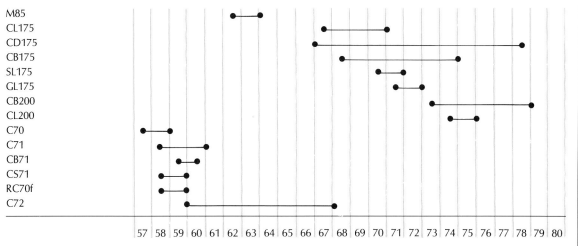

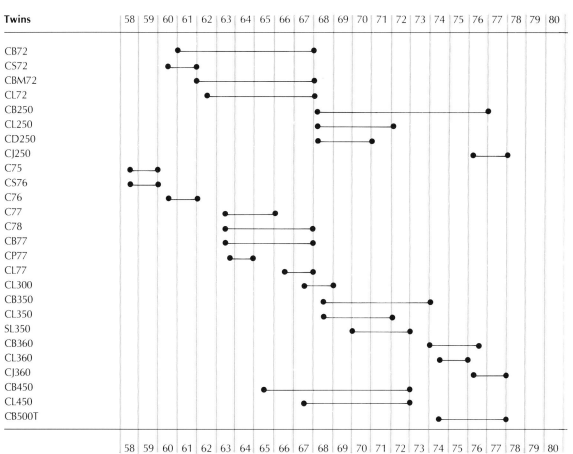

Fours	68	69	70	71	72	73	74	75	76	77	78	79	80
CB750	●		K0	K1	K2	K3	K4	K5	K6	K7	K8		
CB750F								F/F1	F1	F2	F2/F3		
CB750A									●				
CB650													→
CB550							●	K1	K2	K3	K3		
CB550F								F1	F1	F1/F2	F2		
CB500				●									
CB400F							●	F1	F1	F1	F2		
CB350					●								
GL1000							●						
	68	69	70	71	72	73	74	75	76	77	78	79	80

Production road racers	59	60	61	62	63	64	65	66	67	68	69	70	71
CR71													
125 race kit													
CR110													
CR93													
CR72													
CR77													
CYB350													
CR750													
	59	60	61	62	63	64	65	66	67	68	69	70	71

" There's nothing in the regs. about it and he insists it's 49—so I don't see what we can do !"